Colchester's Secret
Roman River

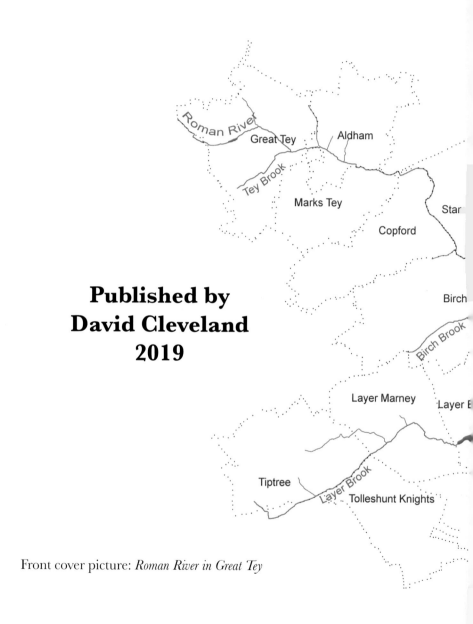

Published by
David Cleveland
2019

Front cover picture: *Roman River in Great Tey*

Colchester's Secret
ROMAN RIVER

Ken Rickwood

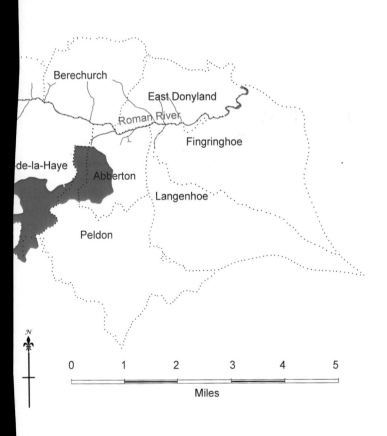

Berechurch

East Donyland

Roman River

Fingringhoe

de-la-Haye

Abberton

Langenhoe

Peldon

N

| 0 | 1 | 2 | 3 | 4 | 5 |

Miles

Published by
David Cleveland
Manningtree, Essex

ISBN   978-1-9993672-2-0

First published December 2019

British Library Cataloguing-in-Publication Data
A catalogue record for this book is available from
The British Library

Designed by Ken Rickwood
Printed in England by Lavenham Press Ltd

CONTENTS

ACKNOWLEDGEMENTS

This book would not have been possible without the help of many people, past and present. I have consulted many books and those listed in the bibliography have all provided me with useful information, but many more have provided an odd snippet here and there. I am indebted to the many individuals who have helped me and I hope that if I fail to mention a name, where I should, it will be forgiven. I have found that most villages have an enthusiastic local historian, many of whom have helped me a great deal. There are also several village web sites maintained by local enthusiasts; the Layer Breton site contains a mine of information about the village and the neighbouring parishes.

I have tried to ascertain the copyright of all the pictures that I have used and included an attribution where appropriate, those unattributed are either in my own collection or photographs I have taken during my travels researching this book.

Individuals and organisations whose help I would like to acknowledge are; Gill Adams, Chris Behn, Simon Brooks, Richard Browning, John Carr, David Cleveland, Colchester Library, Tim Dennis, Christina Edwards, Essex Record Office, Fingringhoe Recorders, Ken Free, Roy Fulcher, Les King, Mersea Museum, Nikki Lax, Joan Pinch, Rowhedge Heritage Trust, Tiptree Museum, Tony Millatt, Geoff Russell Grant, Pete Wakeling, Ros Watling, Mary & Rob Williamson.

INTRODUCTION

Roman River meandering down from Fingringhoe Mill to its confluence with the Colne at Wivenhoe. 1920

Roman River is small and beautiful; she lies hidden in North East Essex. In Willow Wood there is a spring whose clear waters spring forth into a trickle that soon becomes a stream, which is joined by several others that together over many millennia have carved a narrow, steep sided valley twelve miles long across the flatlands of the region.

The valley was explored by our Stone Age forebears who have left a scattering of lost axe heads and other tools. It was not until the Iron Age that the local inhabitants recognized the potential qualities of the steep sides of the valley to both assist in the corralling of their livestock and as a defence against the chariots of neighbouring tribes. Over the years the importance and management of the valley increased until the Roman invasion by which time it was the southern boundary of the most significant settlement in pre-Roman Britain, Camulodunum.

This was the stronghold of Cunobelin who, at the time, was the most powerful tribal leader in southern Britain. His fortified homestead at Gosbecks was within the five square-miles or so of fertile territory that was Camulodunum. This fertile and relatively flat inland promontory was bounded to the north and east by the River Colne and its salt marshes, to the south by Roman River, and to the west by a series of dykes. These would have formed an almost continuous barrier between the two rivers. The Roman River valley could well have been managed but the absence of any additional earthworks parallel to it suggests its natural contours were barrier enough.

Iron Age Camulodunum, an area of some five square-miles defended by Roman River, the River Colne and 12-miles of man-made dykes.

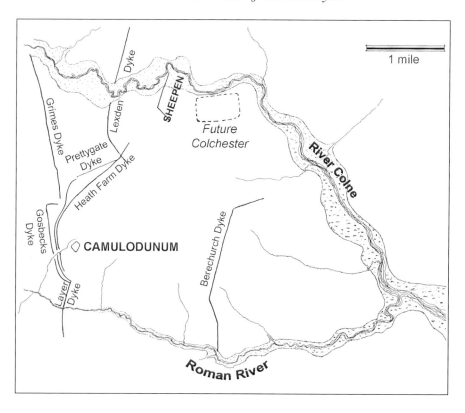

The name of the River Colne is thought to be derived from a Celtic word that simply means water. This river's longest and most significant tributary almost certainly had a Celtic name. We have no clue as to what it was; it may have been another word for water or any of the characteristics of the valley or the spirits thought to inhabit it.

Many of the names of places we will encounter during our exploration of the valley are of Saxon origin. And as for the river itself, it is thought that it is named, not after the Romans, but a family of local landowners, the Romaynes. They were first recorded in the Colchester Court Rolls of 1377.

Roman River rises in the parish of Great Tey, flows through Aldham and Eight Ash Green, Marks Tey, Copford, Stanway, Birch, Layer-de-la-Haye, Berechurch and Langenhoe before arriving at its confluence with the Colne between East Donyland and Fingringhoe. On the way it is joined by its two principle tributaries, Birch Brook and Layer Brook, which flow through the additional parishes of Abberton, Peldon, Layer Breton, Layer Marney, Tolleshunt Knights and Tiptree.

This makes up a catchment area of some 24 square-miles, which I will explore using some of its numerous byways and footways. All the walks described can be followed most easily by using Ordnance Survey (OS) Explorer maps 184, 183 and 195.

Each chapter or section includes a map showing most features mentioned in the text. Those shown in italics indicate a feature which has since disappeared.

This coin, minted in Colchester(CAM) sometime between AD 20-43 carries a likeness of Cunobelin.

CHAPTER 1

East Donyland

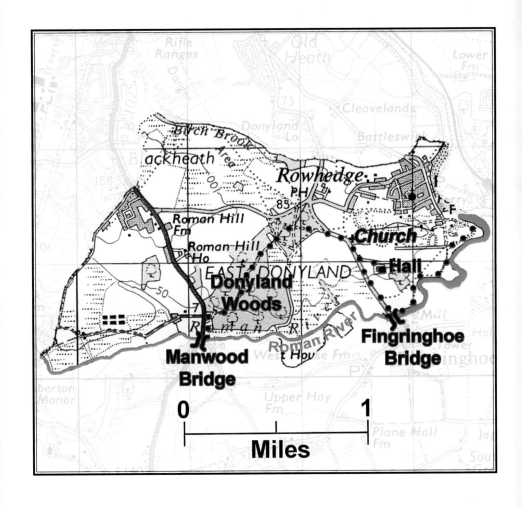

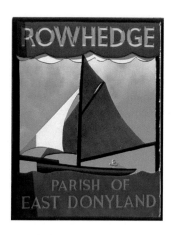

The parish sign displays the ever increasing importance of the riverside settlement of Rowhedge whose name is displayed in larger letters than that of the parish and is represented by the boat, one of the large fleet of fishing smacks that once sailed from the port. Represented in its full sailing rig of forestaysail and jib in front of the mast and mainsail with topsail behind.

The name East Donyland means the eastern quarter of the land that was once controlled by the Saxon named Dunna. Over the years Dunna's land has become Donyland.
Rowhedge is derived from either a 'rough hedge' beyond which this settlement developed or 'rough edge' as a description of edge of the parish as it descended into the River Colne and Roman River

Recorded in the Domesday Book in 1086 as being within the Lordship of Count Eustace of Boulogne formerly held by Edric. Part now held by Godric of Colchester.

In 1848 William White described Donyland (East) as a parish of about 1400 acres and 793 inhabitants with the village of Rowhedge and about fifty fishing boats.

The population of the parish of East Donyland in 2011 was 1930.

When I stood on this spot six years ago it was full of emptiness. There were no ships moored to the rusting bollards, the quay's warehouses had been demolished and scruffy tufts of grass topped by expanding Buddleia were beginning to colonise the cracks in the hard standing. At the end of the concrete a rarely trodden path followed the diminutive sea wall. The line of trampled grass showed that I was not the first to venture along the riverbank of Roman River.

It is now the summer of 2018 and some of the new waterfront properties are occupied. They are set back from the water's edge by a narrow strip of grass and a neatly paved area that runs along the edge of the former wharf. The Roman River path is yet to be put in the straitjacket of the 21st century; I hope that it is left room to breathe. The path along the sea wall is now well trodden by the increased population but the developer's fences appear to be nudging it into the river.

This is where I am starting my exploration of Roman River. Here its waters mingle with those of the River Colne and those of salt from the ebb and flow of the North Sea. Across the Colne is Wivenhoe and across Roman River is Fingringhoe and I am in the parish of East Donyland. Today this is a civil parish; there is no village bearing the name and the parish church is long gone. Only the gravestones remain sentinel in their ancient churchyard. Donyland has a long history. It is an area of land thought to have been associated with a Saxon person called Dunna. Over time Dunna's land or Dunnaland became Donyland. It is likely to have been a considerable area that stretched from the Roman walls of Colchester all the way to Roman River, bounded to the east by the Colne and extending westward as far as Stanway. During the 10th century it was divided into four. Subsequent records are far from clear but it appears three of the quarters became parishes within Colchester, which at various times have been described as being wholly or partly in West Donyland.

East Donyland hung on to its identity until the 18th century when the settlement around the hall and church dwindled as the Colneside area beyond the *'rough hedge'* or Rowhedge began to expand. This is now in the midst of further expansion as new residential developments grow on its former industrial and maritime sites. These are not advertised as being in East Donyland; the area is described as Rowhedge Wharf.

The fence hiding the residential development of Rowhedge Wharf. 2018

After a quarter-mile or so I come to the end of the building site and the fence gives way to a hedge as the path enters a nature conservation area. The path through here is as I remembered it; brambles and sloes tangle below the occasional ancient oak as it follows the twists and turns of the river's meanders up to Fingringhoe Mill. The mill is now divided into apartments and the building is undergoing exterior maintenance. It stands astride the river and the parish boundary. A little below the mill the path divides; either crossing the river where it joins the lane leading up into Fingringhoe village, which I will visit later; the other staying on the East Donyland side to follow the side of the former millpond. It was clear from the overgrown state of the path as it passed the mill that few people choose the Donyland route.

On entering the nature Conservation Area, the riverside path is atop the seawall. 2018

The millpond still rises and falls with the tide but this is now choked with reeds, which restricts the flow and the upstream meadows are liable to flood.

The millpond is bounded by the road bridge that carries Furneaux Lane over Roman River. In 1610 this was called Millbridge when its maintenance was the joint responsibility of Fingringhoe and East

Donyland. It appears that from 1645 the county assumed responsibility and maintained it until it was replaced with a new wooden bridge in 1814. This was a well-built structure supported on five massive trestles, cross-braced between the uprights and with head-pieces projecting beyond the planked deck. It lasted for over a hundred years and was

Towards Fingringhoe Mill. 2018

probably the last surviving wooden bridge in Essex. It was not replaced by another structure until 1923. This was made of Cement Fondu; this is a cement made from limestone and the aluminium ore, bauxite. In 1923 this was a relatively new material developed and patented in France less than fifteen years earlier.

This concrete structure did not last nearly as long as its wooden predecessor. Due largely to the increased volume and weight of the traffic using it. It was planned to replace the central span and parapet in 2004. This exercise took considerably longer than the anticipated nine months due to the fact that once the bridge was

The path just before it divides between the tarmac up to the village or the thicket to the millpond. 2018

closed, demolition was halted and did not resume for many weeks, when a pair of swallows were found to be nesting under the central span. Work was not resumed until the young had fledged.

Fingringhoe Recorders

The old Fingringhoe Bridge built in 1814. It is supported on five massive trestles, cross-braced between the uprights and with head-pieces projecting beyond the planked deck.

The Fingringhoe Bridge built of cement fondu in 1923

Fingringhoe Recorders

Fingringhoe Recorders

Fingringhoe Bridge when demolition was delayed by nesting swallows. 2004

Fingringhoe Bridge with the new central span. 2012

Upstream from the bridge the land is owned by the Ministry of Defence (MoD) This is marked by a Boundary Stone (BS) marked with broad arrow and the letters WD, War Department which, in 1964, became the MoD. 2019

I walked the short way up the hill to East Donyland Hall; a much-modified early 17th century moated, timber-framed house.

The first record of a house on this site dates from 1463 when the rector was accused of 'fishing in the lord's fish ponds at Donyland Hall'. By 1638 the house was recorded as a mansion, entirely surrounded by a moat. Within a few years the Civil War was raging and Donyland Hall was far from quiet. Hundreds of musket balls have been found on the field by the drive; and when the moat was dredged in the 1980s it was found to contain over 2000 more along with a number of cannon balls.

The hall underwent a major face-lift when David Gansel purchased it in 1730. Mr Gansel fancied himself as an amateur architect. He encased the wooden building in brick, creating a stately seven bay façade with rusticated quoins; its size exaggerated by the narrow windows and a deep parapet with false windows that hid the dormers of the attic storey. He built a model farm with stables, dairy and brew house; and set his desirable gentleman's residence in acres of a newly laid-out parkland with fifty cedar trees.

East Donyland Hall as designed by David Gansel. 1900

East Donyland Hall as it appeared after restoration carried out during the 1940s.

Fingringhoe Recorders

The house suffered considerable damage in the 'Great English Earthquake' of 1884 when, it is thought the whole of the North Wing was so badly damaged it was demolished. It appears the property suffered further decline until Captain Lindsey-Smith acquired it in 1943. He restored the derelict farm buildings, and improved the appearance of the house by lowering the parapet to reveal the dormer windows.

Adjoining the grounds of the Hall is the churchyard, the site of the mediaeval church of St Lawrence. On the other side of the road is the footpath I take onto Donyland Heath. This former heath is now indistinguishable from the adjoining Donyland Woods. This is an attractive area of mixed woodland criss-crossed with footpaths and bridleways, many of which are not recorded on any map. Also the paucity of contours on the map does not do justice to its undulations.

East Donyland churchyard, the church once stood at the centre of this view.

*The mediaeval church of St Lawrence comprised a small chancel and nave with a bellcote.
It was demolished in 1840. From a painting of 1816*

Donyland Heath has lost many of the characteristics of impoverished heath land soil. It has disappeared along with the many other heaths that used to ring Colchester shown on early maps. We will come across two of the remaining heaths further along the valley.

I emerged from Donyland Woods at the parish boundary that follows Mersea Road close to where Roman River is crossed by Manwood Bridge.

Strictly speaking Manwood Bridge, along with Man Wood and Manwood Farm are in the parish of Langenhoe. As I am here I will mention what little I know about the bridge. Manwood Bridge is shown on the first definitive map of Essex, surveyed by Chapman & Andre and published in 1777, but there are written records indicating the existence of a bridge from far earlier times. The bridge is first mentioned in the County Records in 1602, when it was ordered *'to be*

One of the many paths through Donyland Wood. 2019

The entrance to Donyland Wood from Mersea Road near Manwood Bridge. 2019

made'; possibly this was a replacement for an earlier structure that had collapsed or perhaps before this date the crossing was merely a ford.

This was clearly regarded as an important river crossing because, although it was indisputably in the parish of Langenhoe, in 1749 no less than another seven parishes were persuaded to contribute to the cost of building a new brick bridge. And again in 1775 the same eight parishes of Abberton, East Mersea, West Mersea, Great Wigborough, Little Wigborough, Peldon, Fingringhoe and Langenhoe were charged with its repair. This was probably the two span brick structure that was replaced in 1893 by a new iron girder bridge. The road was straightened and the bridge replaced by the existing precast concrete structure in the 1960s.

Vehicles now swoop down and over the bridge at speeds that could imperil the lives of the occupants. When the pace of life was slower the

Manwood Bridge, the iron girder structure, erected in 1893, replaced a narrow brick bridge of two spans. c1900

Fingringhoe Recorders

dangers were different. On 24th October 1789 Samuel Deeks and his wife a happy, young couple from Abberton and their friend Sheppard Stammers were returning on horseback from Colchester Market in the early evening. Samuel and his wife were on the same horse and as they were making their way up the hill from the bridge past Manwood three highwaymen emerged from the wood. One, brandishing a pistol at them, demanded their money. Mr Deeks handed over his money but even so the villain fired the pistol. The ball passed close to Samuel's face leaving burn marks on his cheek and throat before passing through his shoulder and then becoming lodged in his wife's head. Despite the offer of a considerable reward no arrests were ever made for the murder of Mrs Deeks.

Before I venture across the bridge and into the wood from which the bridge takes its name I am going to return to Fingringhoe Mill to walk up into the village from where I will follow the river along its southern side back to Manwood.

Below left: Manwood Bridge. Haye Lane entering from the right with Donyland Wood over the bridge, marked by the white pole from which a red flag flies when the Army are firing. Many who drive over this widened bridge are unaware of its existence. 2018

Below right: The 1960s reinforced concrete Manwood Bridge. 2018

16

CHAPTER 2

Fingringhoe

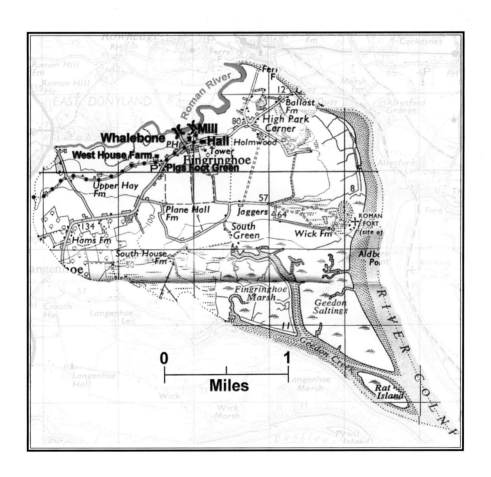

The village sign depicts the church flanked by the Whalebone public house and the Manor house with the mill and bridge. All in a rural scene held in a frame in the shape of its famous oak tree.

The name Fingringhoe is of Saxon origin. Fingringho is mentioned in a will of 975. It could be the old word for a ridge of high ground, hoo, how, hou or hoe either belonging to the Saxon called Fingrigeas or may mean a finger of land that juts out into the Colne.

There is no entry for Fingringhoe in the Domesday Book.

In 1848 William White described Fingringhoe as a pleasant village on the south side of the Roman River, and the west side in the vale of the Colne. The parish contains 581 souls and 2863 acres of land.

The population of the parish of Fingringhoe in 2011 was 775.

I am now back at Fingringhoe Mill, the first crossing place on Roman River. It is now a footpath that crosses on the downstream side of the converted mill. The first road bridge across is now upstream a few hundred yards just beyond the tidal millpond.

The earliest record of a mill on this site dates from 1531 when it was described as 'the newly built mill by Richard Whiter and Robert Cooper'. It is likely that the section of building that straddles the river incorporated timbers from this mill when it was completely rebuilt in 1750. By 1848 a granary had been added and, in 1893, a coal powered steam roller-mill was built alongside the tide mill. This was later converted to oil in 1933 and then to electricity in 1938. The mill was still deriving some of its power from the tide until the early 1940s when the wheels finally stopped turning. The mill prospered longer than most by adopting the speciality of producing cooked flaked maize. This kept the mill working until 1993 when, after over 450 years, all milling finally ceased and the mill was closed. Fortunately before the buildings fell into a state beyond repair they were given listed status and in 1996 work started on converting them to residential use.

Fingringhoe Mill is one of the five mills and the only tide mill known to have been built on Roman river. Harnessing the energy of the tide has always been a fascinating challenge. Nowadays when the effects of global warming and the consequences of over reliance on fossil fuels are becoming ever more apparent, it is surprising that more effort is not made into developing ways of harnessing the energy available from the regular and predictable rise and fall of the tide. The principle is ancient and there are many tide mills recorded in the Domesday Book but the Fingringhoe Mill is not one of these. The earliest record of there being a mill on this site dates from 1531 and was rebuilt during the 18th century when sea-borne transport was becoming important. This led to the enlargement of many existing tide mills and the building of new ones. It also led to the development of many ingenious ways of overcoming the restriction of the limited working hours of most of these mills. It is thought that Fingringhoe Mill would have been able to work three or four hours from half ebb to low water; and these hours would get an hour later every day, necessitating some night shifts every other week. Systems were developed that could keep the mill wheel turning twenty-four hours a day; indeed one was in operation in Liverpool from 1796 until 1827. There are no records of any of these innovative ideas being used at Fingringhoe. These systems were abandoned with the arrival of steam-driven auxiliary engines, a development that was taken up at Fingringhoe Mill.

Sailing barge unloading grain at Fingringhoe Mill when it was still deriving at least some of its power from the tide. 1935

Fingringhoe Recorders

I walked up Mill Lane to Church Road and along to the village centre. Here we have all the elements of the quintessential English village: church, pub, green, pond and hall. It is no wonder that the centre of this village is classified as a conservation area.

Few churches can boast the combination of setting and architectural features present in St Andrew's Fingringhoe. Pevsner described it as 'visually quite exceptionally exceptional' and Scarfe in his guide to Essex as 'irresistibly beautiful' The building is mainly 15th century brick and stone with a tall, attractive west tower of knapped flint and stone.

Opposite the church is the hall. This is a largely modern structure, built after the 17th century building suffered a disastrous fire in 1976. It is thought this building was built on the site of an earlier Tudor manor house. The hall has had many owners in its long history and spent several years as no more than a farmhouse. Close by, within the grounds of Hall Farm stands a large brick tower. This was built as a dovecote sometime during the 18th century. Over the years, a variety of stories of smuggling and bears have been associated with the building. When by the 1980s it had become ruinous and was in danger of disappearing a group of villagers campaigned to save their local landmark. With the help of the Roman River Society, Essex County Council, Colchester Borough Council and numerous other groups and individuals a restoration programme was initiated.

When the top half of the building had been cleared of its years of accumulated debris it was found to contain brick and wooden pigeon nesting holes. Here the young birds would have been fed by their parents and ended up with more meat on them than the adult birds. Then, just before they fledged they were taken for the pot.

The ground floor is a domed chamber which, it is claimed, sits above a brick-lined former bear pit. I have also heard it said the tower was built as a lookout point, giving views along the River Colne estuary,

Fingringhoe Recorders

The partially collapsed roof of Fingringhoe Dovecote before restoration. 1991

Fingringhoe Recorders

Fingringhoe Dovecote restored. 1992

presumably in connection with smuggling activities. This story may be true or could have arisen from the fact the tower is shown on early OS maps as a '*Telegraph Tower (disused)*'.

Telegraph is one of those words whose meaning has appeared to have changed over the years. Its meaning is simple; it is any method or device for transmitting information over a distance. The earliest telegraphs were visual using fire as either beacons or a means of creating smoke signals. The best-known use of such a system in England is the fire beacon system employed to give warning of the approach of the Spanish Armada. Many of the hills on which these beacons stood are remembered by the name Beacon Hill.

Similarly, the name Telegraph Hill commemorates the use of the newly invented telegraphic system of communication at the time when

England feared an invasion by Napoleon. The Admiralty adopted an overland route of visual communication stations between London and its major ports. Also by 1812 there were a series of coastal stations stretching from Deal to Yarmouth with vessels moored in the Thames and Colne to ensure continuity. It is possible the Fingringhoe Telegraph Tower was a support station in this network. Communication between stations was carried out by various means. The simplest involved the raising and lowering of flags. Then there was the shutter system; each station was equipped with a large vertical frame containing a number of shutters, which could be opened or closed to create a variety of patterns each of which had a particular meaning. This enabled quite complicated messages to be conveyed easily and quickly. An alternative, mechanically simpler system utilized movable arms or semaphores. It was the name of the arm or semaphore that was subsequently used to

The 17th century Fingringhoe Hall. c1970

Fingringhoe Recorders

distinguish these early forms of optical communication from the later invented electric, cable or wireless non-visual methods.

It is not known with certainty which, if any of these optical communication systems was used at the Fingringhoe telegraph tower.

Close by the church is the pub, the *Whalebone*. This has been in existence since at least 1735. It was refurbished in the early 19th century and has undergone several 20th century alterations. It has been suggested that, despite the image on the sign and presence of a whale bone on the premises at various times during its life, the name could have been derived from the Saxon word 'valbon' meaning welcome.

Between the pub and the church are two more features of the village centre that are worthy of note. Firstly the oak tree that has such a setting and girth that it is certain to have been the subject of stories

The disastrous fire of 7th January 1976 when one of the occupants, Dorothy Slowgrove fell victim to the blaze.

Fingringhoe Recorders

and legends for a very long time. The village story is that the tree is supposed to have grown from an acorn placed in the mouth of a pirate who had been hanged in the village. It is thought that this may be based on a folk myth dating back to the time of the Danish invaders of the Dark Ages. The present tree is of unknown age but probably dates back to around 1500.

Secondly, beside the oak tree is the village pond, this was once of great importance, not only to Fingringhoe but also to several neighbouring villages. The spring that feeds this pond was the source of the most highly regarded water in the area. For those further afield who could not collect their own water, it was delivered by pony and trap at a cost of a halfpenny a bucket. Then in the 1970s health inspectors deemed the water not fit to drink and the spring head now carries a warning sign. I am not sure if there is a real health risk or if this is more to provide a defence in the case of possible litigation.

The rebuilt Fingringhoe Hall. 2019

The Whalebone *at the crossroads in the centre of Fingringhoe. 2012*

The view down the hill from here reveals the bridge that crosses the river just above the millpond, which I described earlier. Now, I am going back to the *Whalebone* and along Abberton Road to a small triangle of grass, Pig's Foot Green. Here, in the shade of an oak tree, is a seat and an anvil, which bears a plaque with the inscription '*Presented by W B Fookes, the last of his family who had been blacksmiths since before 1470 at the forge situated opposite this green.*'

Over the years the many customers visiting the forge would have travelled along one of three unmade roads that met at the green. Today only one of these roads remains unsurfaced and this, Upper Hay Lane follows most closely Roman River Valley. At the beginning of the lane stands West House Farm and the adjacent farmhouse, which is no longer part of the farm and is now known as Old West House.

> *The Parish Council of Fingringhoe*
>
> *This anvil was presented in 1980
> by W. B. Fookes, who was the last
> of his family who had been
> blacksmiths since before A.D.1470
> at a forge situated opposite
> this green.*

A memorial to the family of blacksmiths who operated the village forge from 1470 to 1980 on Pig's Foot Green. 2019

This house was for many years home to generations of the Page family and the lane itself is known to older locals as Page's Chase. Much information can be gleaned about life and farming in Fingringhoe at the end of the 18th century from the diaries written by Joseph Page.

Joseph farmed West House Farm during the Napoleonic Wars when high food prices brought great prosperity to Essex farmers. During this period Joseph not only earned enough to increase the size of his 30-acre farm, support his wife and three children along with a household of domestic servants, but also had sufficient time to avail himself of his numerous opportunities for sport and entertainment. All on an income estimated by Income Tax officials of £80 a year.

West House Farmhouse. c1920

Old West House, the former West House Farmhouse which had a Georgian façade concealing what was thought to be a Tudor hall house. 2018

View across Roman River from Upper Haye Lane. 2018

I proceeded along the unmade lane, catching glimpses over hedges and through gateways of fine views of the meandering valley, until I reached Upper Hay Farm. This sits in a commanding position overlooking the fields, meadows and woodland of the valley but the farm itself, its buildings and farmhouse are in a sorry state.

Beyond the farmhouse the track crosses Haye Lane, which descends to Mersea Road where it crosses Roman River at Manwood Bridge; but the unmade road continues straight on. Now designated as a public footpath the track goes as far as Hay Farm. This sits at the western extremity of the parish and from here the track becomes a path across a field that slopes steeply down to one of the many minor tributaries of Roman River. This stream, no more than a few hundred yards long, flows in a well-delineated valley and is the parish boundary between Fingringhoe and Langenhoe. The path crosses the stream by a simple plank bridge guarded by a stile, which I cross and I am in the parish of Langenhoe.

The Georgian façade of the much older, somewhat neglected Upper Haye Farmhouse. 2018

One of the derelict Upper Haye Farm barns. 2018

CHAPTER 3

Langenhoe

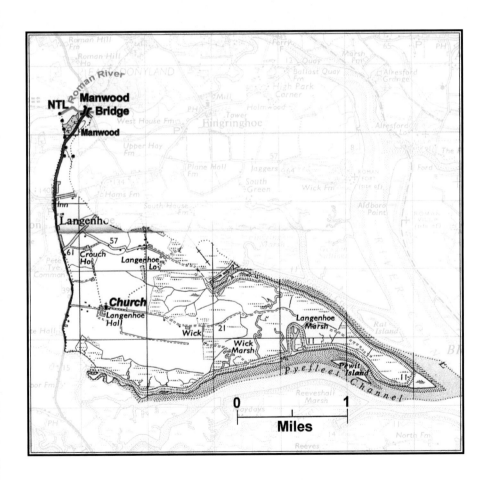

Langenhoe village sign is amalgamated with that of Abberton and is dominated by the reservoir, its pumping station and wildlife. Langenhoe is primarily a farming community, represented by corn and other crops in the surround. The watery coast by the wavy underlining of its name.

It is generally agreed the name Langenhoe is derived from the Old English word 'Lang-hou' meaning long spur or long hill.

Recorded in the Domesday Book in 1086 as being within the Lordship of Count Eustace of Boulogne formerly held by Engelric. It contained one mill and one salt house.

In 1848 William White described Langenhoe as a scattered village on a declivity. It has 161 inhabitants and about 2063 acres extending to the river Colne with a further 30 acres of waste and water.

The population of the parish of Langenhoe in 2011 was 572.

The early parish of Langenhoe was much longer than it is today. At one time a finger of the parish extended to the north of Roman River. For many centuries the village was centered around the church which was well to the south of the present settlement that has now become amalgamated with Abberton. There have been enormous changes; the population has moved, the church demolished and the parish boundary altered. In 1946 the remaining remnants of the parish north of Roman River were transferred to East Donyland.

Parish boundaries have always been subject to change. Christianity was first practiced in England by a few during the Roman occupation and a small minority continued to practice through the turbulent times following the Roman withdrawal. Then some hundreds of years later when things had settled down Christianity took hold and was practiced by royalty and many noblemen. Then during the 10th century some lords of the manors provided chapels on their land where those living within their manor could use the services of a priest. The manorial territory associated with its chapel soon became regarded by the Church authorities as an administrative area and was called a parish. Some present day parish boundaries can be traced back to these early manorial boundaries. These often followed natural features such as rivers or Roman roads. A further complication was that the manors themselves were not static. Inheritance and marriage meant some were amalgamated, some disappeared and others acquired lands detached from the original manor. The parish as an administrative area became responsible for maintaining order within its boundaries. To do this it collected 10% of everyone's earnings, known as a tithe. This provided for the upkeep of the church, the recording of births, marriages and deaths, provision for the poor, maintenance of roads and so on.

As the role of the manor diminished some parish boundaries were rationalised and then a major change occurred during the mid 19th century when the existing ecclesiastical parish boundaries were used to create a network of civil parishes. These became responsible for civil matters previously handled by the church. These new civil parishes were administered as the lowest tier of local government. Today, these civil parishes, just like their predecessors, are not static. Their boundaries move and new ones are created, often due to population movement and growth.

It did not take me long to cross the two fields along the rarely used path to emerge though a hedge on to the Mersea Road. I had crossed the parish, which at this point is less than 200 yards wide. This road is also the ancient parish boundary between Langenhoe and Abberton and is one that was likely to have been established along the course of the Roman road that connected Colchester to Mersea. It is along here that the names of these two parishes appear on the same village sign. The parish boundary is along the middle of this road which means that those travelling towards Colchester pass through Abberton but those going in the opposite direction pass through Langenhoe.

Yet this quiet nondescript parish did enjoy a short-lived period of fame when pictures of its church appeared in the national papers. This was in 1884 when Langenhoe was close to the epicentre of the strongest earthquake to strike mainland Britain. Of the twenty churches damaged by the event the one to sustain the most dramatic damage was at Langenhoe. A report at the time stated: '*The Reverend Parkinson was sitting in the rectory when the earthquake struck. He felt "a violent shock." The whole house shook for a few seconds shattering the chimneys, cracking ceilings and collapsing part of the roof. On emerging from the rectory, the Reverend beheld the sad sight of the church. "It seemed utterly ruined" he later said, "some tons of the stone battlements of the tower had been dislodged. These had fallen with great force upon the nave, which was almost entirely destroyed." The interior*

The interior and exterior of Langenhoe Church after the earthquake of 22 April 1884.

Colchester Library Collection

suffered further still. "Roof timbers and masonry had smashed the pews and pulpit. The altar was buried under debris and the choir gallery had been ripped from its wall foundations."'

For a while Langenhoe Church was known as the *'Earthquake Church'*. The damage was so severe that the whole building was demolished and rebuilt using much of the old stone and original material. The 15th century windows and doorways were re-used and the 500-year-old doors were rehung, as was the bell. All this was accomplished in two years and the new church was re-opened in 1886.

Its troubles were far from over as it later acquired the reputation as one of the most haunted places in England. This was as a result of a number of disturbing happenings experienced by the Reverend Ernest Merryweather who was rector there for twenty years. Many of these could be attributed to a combination of a poor quality rebuild and the interpretation by the rector of 'things that go bump in the night'. Never the less, the last service was held in 1959 and the church was closed. The reason given at the time was that the building was too dangerous. This prompted a BBC ghost hunting team to spend the night there in 1961. Absolutely nothing happened! Meanwhile the authorities decided that funds were not available for the necessary repairs to the dangerous building so plans for demolition were put in place. This was carried out in 1962, a mere 76 years after being rebuilt. The parish of Langenhoe was united with Abberton and the Parish Council still maintain the graveyard.

I walked along the main road the short distance to Man Wood, which I entered through a metal kissing gate. The path took me straight down through the wood to emerge onto a water meadow a few yards upstream from Manwood Bridge. The path is ill-defined over the close-cropped pasture to the riverbank and a footbridge. This bridge is marked on the map as NTL. This is one of the less common signs that appear on OS maps. It means Normal Tidal Limit. This may well have been the case at the time of the survey but since then the river has become considerably more choked and I have failed to detect any tidal movement this far upstream.

As I cross the bridge I find myself back in my first parish of East Donyland. The path takes me across the meadow to Ball Lane. This runs parallel to the river through what is now MoD land, to the shuttered and barred buildings of the former Rock Farm, which is also in the hands of the MoD. The lane that is now no more than a track turns right into the unmade Cherry Tree Lane, which is the boundary into my next parish, the former Berechurch, now part of Colchester District.

The footpath through Man Wood with the discrete sign from the Country Landowners Association to remind walkers to keep to the footpath. 2018

Footbridge over Roman River at what the map describes as its Normal Tidal Limit (NTL) 2018

CHAPTER 4

Berechurch

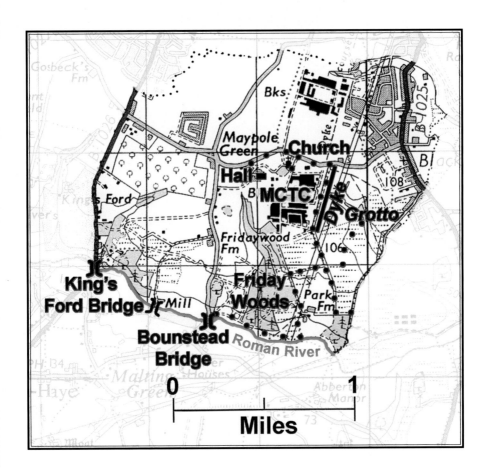

There is no longer a village or parish and the pub sign which is not in the former parish carries the arms of Colchester of which it is now a part.

The earliest record of the name from which Berechurch is derived dates from 1170.

This has been variously interpreted as Beordescherche, which means 'church in the cornfields' or Berdechirche meaning 'a church made of boards.

There is no entry for Berechurch or West Donyland in the Domesday Book.

In 1848 William White described Berechurch or West Donyland as a very small parish having 147 inhabitants.

The population of Berechurch ward (Colchester) in 2011 was 9717.

Note: Berechurch is no longer a parish, it is a ward within Colchester. The population is taken from the ward statistics but the map boundary used is the parish as it was in 1898.

Berechurch was formerly known as West Donyland. As was mentioned earlier this was established in the 10th century and occupied a sizeable area of land stretching from the walls of Colchester town all the way to Roman River. Since its inception West Donyland's boundaries have been subject to change. By the Middle Ages it had lost about half of its lands abutting Colchester and since then has continued to shrink. Its southern boundary along Roman River has been its most enduring but even this has been shortened so that by 1846 it extended for only the mile or so between the ford below Rock Farm and Kingsford Bridge.

The decline continued into the 20th century when the remaining agricultural area came under pressure from the expanding built-up area of Colchester. And from 1926 onwards much of the Berechurch Hall estate was gradually acquired by the War Department for military training and housing. Then after WWII the Hall, which had become ruinous, was demolished and St Michael's church was replaced by a new building located to the north in the post-war building development of Monkwick. The whole area had become part of Colchester District. Never the less I will wander along to the site of the former hall to see what there is left to see.

I have been wandering this area for many years and I remember seeing the boundary stone in the dim and distant past but realized I had not noticed it recently. I had to find it or declare that it was no longer extant. After some time searching, I noticed an old fence post behind a more recent wire fence all entwined within a vigorous growth of ivy. After a little judicious gardening the boundary stone was revealed.

Close by this the lane to the left is barred by a locked gate. There is a side gate for pedestrians; I pull this shut behind me as I pass though. A short way along here the lane turns to the right and becomes increasingly elevated and to my right there is what appears to be a large ditch. The lane is no longer a through route to motor vehicles. It was never very

Berechurch is shown as West Donyland or Bere Church by Chapman & Andre. 1777.

On the 1st edition OS map of 1805 it is simply West Donyland

On the revised edition OS map of 1898 it has become Berechurch.

The post WWII edition OS map of 1956 does not show either.

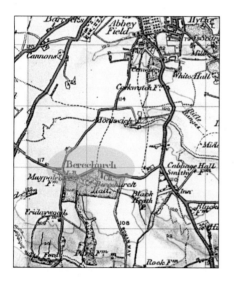

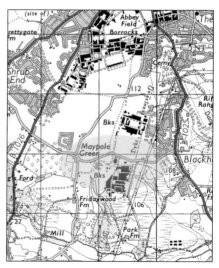

The hidden and revealed boundary stone. 2018

busy and now it is even less so but I notice an increasing number of dog walkers and concomitant numbers cars parked wherever they can get to.

This is in fact Berechurch Dyke, an Iron Age earthwork constructed over 2000 years ago. It was part of the defences of the pre-Roman settlement of Camulodunum. We will get closer to the most accessible parts of this Iron Age settlement a few miles further upstream. For now I am walking along its outermost eastern defences in the footsteps of our Iron Age ancestors. Today, in places, the embankment is over ten feet (3m) high and the dyke several feet deeper. 2000 years ago it would have been considerably higher and the dyke even deeper. It ran all the way from Roman River to the Colne, a distance of over three miles. The bank may have been topped with a wooden palisade. The southernmost mile or so, as far as Berechurch Hall Road, is quite well preserved. To my left there are several paths leading into the area known locally as Friday Woods. I will explore these after visiting St Michael's Church and the site of Berechurch Hall. There are probably more trees now than when this area of fertile land was first cleared. A little further along, almost hidden within the trees, are several single-story red-brick buildings all behind a substantial fence.

These are shown on the map as Berechurch Hall Camp or Barracks. They house the MCTC, the only remaining Military Corrective Training Centre in the UK. The authorities insist this is not a prison but a rehabilitation facility for those who have offended against military law. It has both male and female detainees from the Army, Royal Navy and Royal Air Force. Even so, Her Majesty's Inspectorate of Prisons check the establishment regularly. And many in the armed forces refer to it as the 'Glasshouse'. This term for a military prison originates from the Aldershot Detention Barracks, a multi-story building of Victorian design, which had a large glazed roof.

The Berechurch Hall Camp was never anything like this. The area was first used as a WWII Prisoner of War (PoW) camp. Information concerning PoW camps is difficult to come by. For some reason the military seem to have preserved little of their history. In 1948, when the

The Colchester MCTC site was formerly Prisoner of War Camp No 186 where the detainees were housed in Nissen huts until it closed in 1947. The new accommodation, shown here, for the MCTC was officially opened in 1988.

Red Cross asked for a list of camps they were told it would be impossible to compile a list because, not only have the numbers and locations of camps changed continually, a camp in the same location may have had a succession of different numbers or a camp with the same number may have moved to several different locations. And local newspapers were loath to acknowledge the existence of any camps in their area, presumably due to the need for wartime security. Despite these difficulties, in 2010, Ken Free managed to amass a considerable amount of information about the history of the Berechurch camp and published a book, *Camp 186 – The lost Town of Berechurch*. This is a fascinating account assembled from official sources and contemporary accounts made by the inmates along with stories from their descendents.

At the start of the war there were few PoWs. The small number of survivors captured from ships, submarines and shot-down aircraft were housed in requisitioned, isolated country houses in the northern counties. Although there may have been some thoughts about establishing a camp at Berechurch nothing happened until 1944 when suddenly, following the Normandy landings, there were tens of thousands of surrendered personnel to accommodate.

The multi-story, Victorian Aldershot Detention Barracks, 'The Glasshouse'. 1908

The first consignment of 1500 men arrived during the gloomy night of 19th September 1944. The gates were opened and they were confronted with lines of canvas rolls and poles, dimly illuminated by rows of shaded overhead lamps. Their first task was to erect the tents. The exhausted prisoners slept, twelve in each tent. The following morning they awoke to see they were in a large flat field surrounded by a barbed wire fence. The field contained nothing but the tents they had erected the night before. After some negotiation they were issued with boilers, cooking pots and coal. They managed to set up a make-shift kitchen and by the end of the day all had their first hot meal at Berechurch.

More PoWs arrived every night so that by the end of the week there were over 6000. It is said the food was good and plentiful but it took several weeks to set up adequate cooking facilities. Then there was the winter weather; the rain quickly turned the grass meadow into a sea of mud. And it took until Christmas for permission to be granted for the use of stoves in the tents to help to alleviate the freezing conditions.

Materials for building more substantial accommodation began to arrive a couple of months later. Most of the Nissen Huts housed eighteen men; others were used as kitchens, mess rooms, medical rooms etc. Very soon the PoWs had erected over 1300 buildings and the time-consuming work of construction came to an end; this left time for individuals to pursue their own personal interests. The medical centre was expanded and another hut housed a stage for theatrical productions, and in another there were opportunities for a variety of performing arts. Church groups were formed and the book-reading group led to the establishment of a library, helped with donations from the Red Cross. And, of course, there were arts & crafts and sport. In short a town; the town of Berechurch.

The war ended and repatriation started shortly after in 1946 and was complete by 1948. Colchester Borough Council applied for permission

A photograph of Berechurch Camp taken by the War Office showing the tented camp still in use. By then the first Nissen Huts had been built and are visible in the distance. 1947

©Imperial War Museum (D26737)

to use the site to help relieve the local housing shortage. But it is likely the War Office had already decided the Berechurch site would be used as a Military Corrective Training Centre and military offenders held at other locations were moved in very soon after the Council's request was rejected.

One of several contemporary linocuts made by PoWs showing a view of the Nissen huts at Berechurch Camp.

I have reached Berechurch Hall Road; this has become the unofficial Colchester southern by-pass and is very busy. Fortunately there is a footpath that I followed to the roundabout from where it is but a short distance to the main entrance to MCTC. Adjacent to this is a lane leading to St Michael's Church, now occupied by Martin Elliott & Co, solicitors and b3 architects. St Michael's was declared redundant in 1975 and has since been used for various purposes. That is, apart from the Audley Chapel, which is cared for by the Churches Conservation Trust.

It is possible that there was a church on this site in the 11th century, but the earliest part of the present building is the 14th century tower. In 1536 Thomas Audley, the Lord Chancellor to Henry VIII, was licensed to create a separate rectory at Berechurch, and it is very likely Thomas Audley built the chapel, which now bears his name. It houses

The church of St Michael, Berechurch, from a painting by J Greig, 1824

monuments to several Audleys and to others associated with Berechurch Hall in more recent times. Over the years the church experienced a growing congregation and in 1872 the main body of the church was rebuilt. Then, after WWII the church could not cope with the growing numbers from the nearby new housing estates. This resulted in a new church dedicated to St Margaret being built closer to these new houses and St Michael's was declared redundant.

Thomas Audley would have been able to walk the short distance across the park to his home, Berechurch Hall.

There was probably a hall on this site in the 14th century and by the 16th it must have been substantial. One, Thomas Audley considered stately enough in which to entertain his monarch, Henry VIII and entourage.

The church of St Michael, Berechurch. The Audley Chapel is to the side of the main body of the church. 2018

The house was damaged during the Civil War when it was the home of the royalist Sir Henry Audley. Presumably it was repaired or rebuilt as by 1662 it was recorded that Berechurch Hall had

Above: Monument to sir Henry Audley with images of his five children, three daughters and two sons; the one carrying a skull indicates he had died prior to the building of the monument in 1648.

Left: White marble Memorial to Charlotte White who died in 1845 at the age of 33 She was the beloved daughter of Sir G H Smyth of Berechurch Hall.

twenty hearths. Several subsequent owners made alterations and improvements resulting in a substantial property in the Georgian style. It had a parapeted front of eleven bays with a central pediment and porch.

In 1882 most of the building was demolished and a new house of some 80 rooms was built on the same foundations in red-brick with stone dressings in the domestic French Gothic style. Some rooms, including the dining room and saloon of the Georgian house, were retained. A stable block for 30 horses was built to the west of the house, and new staff houses were built on the estate. The whole house was to be illuminated by gas but the new owner, Octavious Coope, whose name is associated with the Romford brewery, changed his mind and the new Berechurch Hall became the first in the county and one of the first in the country to be illuminated by electricity. The installation was carried out by Crompton, of Chelmsford, who used dynamos manufactured by his own company. These were driven by a steam engine manufactured by Davey Paxman, of Colchester. The power generated was sufficient to illuminate 200 Swan lamps. Berechurch Hall became a national focal point in the ongoing debate between the advocates of gas or electricity. Coope's impartiality, along with his meticulous recording of the performance of the system, played a large part in the rapid acceptance of the idea of domestic electric lighting.

From 1898 Mrs Frances Hetherington owned the hall. Her son Lieutenant Thomas Hetherington paid her a visit in 1913 in the new Army airship 'Eta', which was piloted by Lieutenant Major the Hon Claude Brabazon. The airship visited Abbey Fields and remained tethered for the night in Berechurch Hall Park. It returned to its base in Farnborough the following day. 'Eta' was the Army's last experimental airship before the Government transferred all airship development from the Army to the Navy.

The Georgian style Berechurch Hall. 1877

Berechurch Hall was rebuilt in 1882 in the French Gothic style. c1905

By 1915 Thomas Hetherington had risen to rank of Flight Commander and was one of three initial members of the Landship Committee whose task was to develop armoured fighting vehicles for use on the Western Front. The codename for the vehicle they developed was the 'Tank' and referred to as Little Willie; it was the first completed tank prototype in history. It is now the oldest surviving individual tank and is in the collection of The Tank Museum, Bovington.

The airship, Eta *in Berechurch Hall Park, the Hall can be seen on the left in the background. 1913*

After 1921 the house was unoccupied until it was requisitioned by the War Department during WWII. It was demolished in 1952 and in 1986 replaced by a building of similar size but comprised of 28 individual residential apartments accessed from a common entrance and communal hallway.

Prior to the occupation of the Hall by Octavious Coope it was lived in the Smyth family. Sir George and Lady Eva's only daughter Charlotte Smyth was born at the Hall in 1813. She was regarded by

Berechurch Hall is now a prestigious apartment block set in attractive grounds. 2018.

all as beautiful, and was doted on by an indulgent father who built her a swimming pool or grotto. At the time the grounds of the hall included several freshwater springs and these produced rivulets that ran down into Roman River. The grotto was built beside one of these streams. Contemporary descriptions describe it as a circular red-brick structure containing three niches beneath a domed roof. Each of the niches was plastered white and ornamented with shells. Curving steps led into an oval pool fed by the freshwater spring and overflowed into the stream.

On her nineteenth birthday Charlotte married and moved some twenty miles away to Wethersfield Manor where her six children were born before her untimely death at the age of thirty-two. Throughout her married life she was a frequent visitor to Berechurch and some say she has never left.

There have been many reports of sightings of 'The Lady in White'. The caretakers of the Hall during the 1920s were so disturbed by these apparitions that they took alternative employment and moved away. There were also reports of several separate sightings by various locals and even some of the PoWs claim to have witnessed the ephemeral 'Lady in White'. Some of these occurred within the hall, others in various places in the grounds, and some at her favourite place, the site of the former grotto. The modern boundaries of the hall, MCTC and Friday Woods would be no barrier to her ethereal spirit. As for me I retraced my route back to Berechurch Dyke and entered Friday Woods in my search for the site of Charlotte's Grotto.

I located where I think it could have been, now no more than a damp depression, partially filled with rubbish and fallen chestnut leaves; it still exudes an air of mystery.

Friday Woods remains an interesting area in which I like to roam. There are many tracks and paths used by the Army as a troop training area and as a popular recreational area for local residents and dog-walkers. When I first visited these woods during the 1950s there were no fences or barriers. But then some folk abused the easy access, which resulted in the installation of barriers to prevent fly tipping and the dumping of abandoned vehicles. Sometime later a car park was provided for visitors. Things worked well for a few years until the location became too popular with inconsiderate dog walkers. The frequency with which troops returned from exercises smeared with deposits left by civilian pet owners became such that action had to be taken for health and safety reasons. The car park was closed and more barriers erected.

I have often wondered why Friday Woods are so called. Local people refer to the area as Friday Woods rather than Friday Wood. I have not seen the plural spelling on any map but Friday Wood occurs on many of them, sometimes more than once and not always in the

The ruins of Charlotte's Grotto. 1926   *Today there are no visible remains. 2019*

same place. Chapman & Andre's map of 1777 indicates just a small area of woodland adjacent to Bounstead Road. Successive editions of subsequent OS maps indicate a progressively expanding area of woodland. So, maybe as the additional area of woodland became incorporated the name changed from the singular to the plural.

As to the name itself, there seems to be no consensus as to its derivation. Up and down the country there are several place names and field names that incorporate the name of the fifth day of the week. Friday is named after the Scandinavian goddess Freyja or her Germanic equivalent Friga. Places named Friday may be associated with a site sacred this goddess. Alternatively, it has been suggested that because Friday was often a day when Christians fasted, the word in a place-name could mean unproductive land, a shunned or out of the way place.

In the case of the Berechurch Friday Wood, I have been unable to find any indication that the area has ever had any spiritual relevance to Freyja. But the early area of the wood may have been restricted to relatively unproductive land. I have found a document in the Essex Record Office written in 1536 that refers to Friday Wood in West

Donyland (Berechurch) that formerly belonged to St Botolph's Priory, Colchester. Maybe to the occupants of the priory, a small wood at the extremity of their possessions in West Donyland would qualify as being unproductive or out of the way. Today these qualities are an asset to the owners, the MoD, and the many folk who visit Friday Woods every year.

From the site of Charlotte's Grotto I made my way down to the river. There is a path that more or less follows its bank as far as Bounstead Bridge. This is where I emerged on to the road and I leave Roman River as it enters the parish of Layer-de-la-Haye.

I wandered back to the southeast corner of Friday Woods which is near the confluence of the river with its longest tributary, Layer Brook which I will explore in the following chapter.

One of the foot bridges that cross Roman River into Friday Woods. 2018

Roman River as it flows through Friday Woods. 2018

CHAPTER 5 i

Abberton

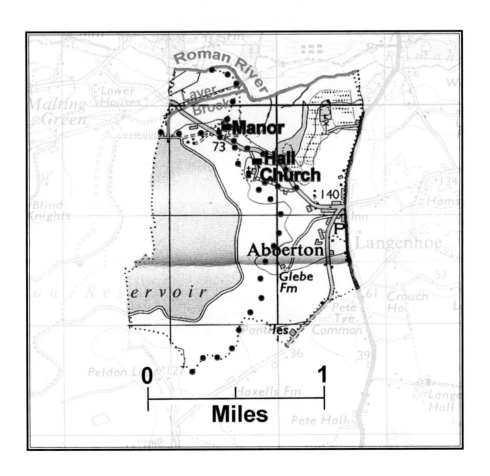

Abberton village sign is amalgamated with that of Langenhoe. It is dominated by the reservoir, the pumping station and wildlife. The symbol used as an ampersand in the form of a white cross on a red background could represent the association with the Knights Templar, although this is usually a red cross on a white background.

It is thought Eadburgh was the name of a Saxon woman and this was her ton or settlement. Then over the years Eadbergh's ton became Abberton.

Recorded in the Domesday Book in 1086 as Edburghetuna and as Edburgetuna in the Hundred of Winstree, when it was part of the lands of Count Eustace in Essex, held by Ralph de Marcy and further held by Ranulf Peverel in demesne; it was held by Siward, a free man, as a manor in the time of King Edward before the Norman conquest of 1066.

In 1848 White describes Abberton as having 248 souls and 1067 acres of strong loamy land, mostly arable. The church of St Andrew stands on a small eminence and is a small plain structure with a brick steeple.

The population of the parish of Abberton in 2011 was 424.

The Layer Brook flows through the parishes of Abberton, Peldon, Layer-de-la-Haye, Layer Breton, Layer Marney, Tolleshunt Knights and Tiptree.

I find it a little odd that Roman River has lost its Celtic name. I am certain it had one. After all it flows into the Colne, which is derived from the Celtic word that means water. And I am about to explore its principle tributary; Layer Brook whose name it is believed is derived from a Celtic word that means marshy. In 1086 it is recorded as Leire Brook. This is certainly an apt description of the ground on which I find myself squelching about. The confluence of Roman River and Layer Brook is somewhere within, the boggy area of long grass and rivulets stretching out in front of me. Over my left shoulder is the bridge, installed by the military not that long ago, that replaced a ford across Roman River. I turn to my right and over that shoulder is a far less conspicuous structure, a grass covered, flat bridge over Layer Brook. This carries a footpath up to Abberton Manor that I can see nestling in the hillside, surrounded by trees that completely obscure the church and Abberton Hall beyond.

The parishes of Layer Brook.

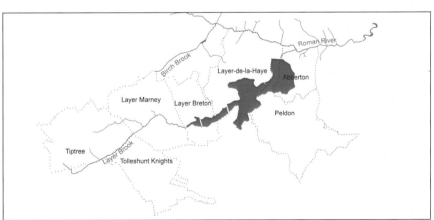

Overgrown ford and choked Roman River near the southeast corner of Friday Wood. I crossover the Bridleway Bridge and enter the parish of Abberton. The boggy area to the left of the bridge is where the water from Layer Brook mingles with that of Roman River.

From the river I have a choice of paths up to the manor. I take the one that leads on to the church. Abberton Manor stands on an ancient site with nearby evidence of Bronze Age occupation. Parts of the existing red-brick house date from the 17th century with extensive alterations made in both the 19th and 20th; the most recent for the conversion of the building into a nursing home with accommodation for 26 residents. Many of the original Queen Anne features have been retained in keeping with the surrounding formal gardens. All are set in several acres of woodland with extensive views over the Roman River Valley.

The path continues past the manor, up the hill, along the road to the lane that leads to the church. The church stands on a site on rising ground that may well have been of earlier religious significance. The church records go back to 1100, but the earliest part of the existing

Abberton Manor from the confluence of Roman River and Layer Brook. 2018

The front of Abberton Manor. 2018

St Andrew's Church, Abberton. 2019

church is the 14th century nave. The rest of the simple building consists of a chancel, porch and 16th century brick tower that contains one bell.

Close by the church is the partially moated site of Abberton Hall. The existing dwelling is a modest 19th century two storey house under a grey slate hipped roof.

The church and the hall overlook Abberton Reservoir that now fills a substantial part of Layer Brook Valley. This is the largest reservoir in Essex and the fourth largest in England. Initially completed in 1939 it underwent significant enlargement in 2015 when its capacity was increased by 58% from 26,000 million litres to 41,000 million litres. Well over half of its surface area of over five square kilometers lies in parish of Layer-de-la-Haye, with smaller areas taken from the parishes of Layer Breton, Peldon and Abberton. Both the visitor centre and

A winter view of Abberton Reservoir from Abberton Church. 2019

the pumping station fall within the parish of Layer-de-la-Haye, and the major part of the retaining dam is in Peldon. I suppose Abberton comes first in the alphabetical list of the parishes the reservoir covers but, apart from this I have yet to find any other reason why this parish name was given to the reservoir.

The story of the reservoir starts in 1934. As a result of several years of drought during the previous decade the South Essex Water Company sought permission to build Abberton Reservoir and Layer-de-la-Haye Treatment Works. Although the reservoir occupies most of Layer Brook valley it is not and never has been filled from this diminutive stream. As part of the project the Water Company built an extraction and pumping station on the River Stour at Stratford St Mary. A pipeline from there could deliver up to 160 million litres a day to the new reservoir, which was completed in 1939.

Then international events took over. It was feared that this new area of water about a mile wide and four times as long could be a landing site for enemy seaplanes. To forestall this possibility 312 mines suspended by cables attached to concrete blocks were installed in reservoir. Other wartime activity at the reservoir were visits from 617 Squadron or *The Dam Busters* who practiced night-time low level flying towards Layer Causeway which, although lacking towers, bore a certain resemblance to the Eder Dam.

At the end of the war, from the banks of the reservoir, soldiers fired at the mines, exploding most of them. The few that sank without exploding were forgotten until the long dry summers in the late 1980s when 22 of these mines were exposed on the reservoir's banks. The Army was called in to finish the job. Since then, a specialist diving unit has carried out a thorough survey and the reservoir has now been declared officially safe.

Although enemy aircraft never flew into the reservoir it has become a popular destination to many other flying aliens. This destination, for the estimated 40,000 migratory birds that visit each year is now regarded to be of such importance that it is protected by UK, European and international organizations. Within the UK it is a Site of Special Scientific Interest (SSSI); under the European Union Directive on the Conservation of Wild Birds it is designated as a Special Protection Area (SPA); and under the Ramsar Convention, an intergovernmental environmental treaty established in 1971, in the Iranian city of Ramsar, by UNESCO it is designated a Ramsar site; that is a wetland site of international importance.

I continued my walk along the path through Abberton churchyard to the road. A short way along here I turned right on to the footpath down to Layer Brook, passing Abberton Manor on my right. I crossed the brook to join the bridleway that follows it upstream. The bridleway follows an ancient field boundary separating the water meadow from the gently rising valley side, now grazed by sheep. There is a gate opening onto the road beyond which is the steeply rising embankment of the reservoir.

At one time the parish of Peldon extended northwards from here as far as Roman River, but with the building of the reservoir this part of the parish between Layer Brook and Roman River would have become detached. The parish boundary now follows the reservoir road along the top of the dam. This means that the part of the parish that occupied the Layer Brook Valley is now submerged.

The slow flowing Layer Brook below Abberton Reservoir, 2018.

Bridge over Layer Brook on Layer Road below Abberton Reservoir, 2018.

CHAPTER 5 ii

Peldon

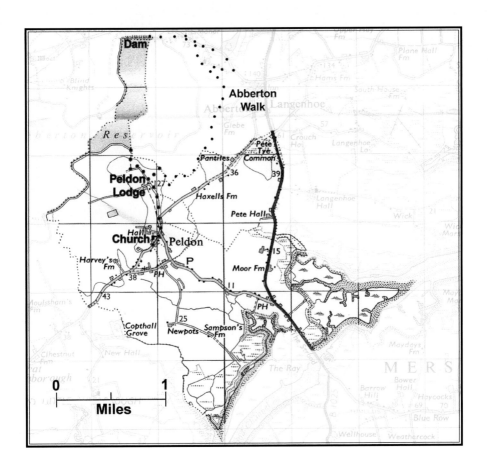

The Peldon sign is crowned by its hilltop church on a foreground representing the two village inns, The Plough and The Peldon Rose.

The name Peldon could be derived from the name of a Saxon, Pylta who owned the hill, dune or dun, hence Pylta's dun, which has had various spellings before becoming Peldon. Alternatively the name could be from the Old English pyltandone, a word that means to thrust up, as the hill appears to do from the surrounding lowland marshes.

Recorded in the Domesday Book in 1086, Peltenduna was held by Odo. Before the conquest the manor, some land and a salt house was owned by Thorkel.

In 1848 White described the parish as containing 493 souls and 2182 acres of land, mostly on a bold acclivity, but descending southward to low salt marshes.

The population of the parish of Peldon in 2011 was 559.

Peldon's principle claim to fame is that it was at the epicentre of the strongest, recorded earthquake to ever strike the UK. It occurred on the 22nd April 1884 and measured 5.1 magnitude on the Richter scale. It damaged more than 1200 buildings over a wide area including, it is said, every single building in Peldon.

The church of St Mary the Virgin sustained only slight damage. Some say the 14th century tower is leaning as a result, and others that it is due to subsidence. It occupies a commanding position overlooking both the Blackwater Estuary and Roman River Valley, and is of Anglo-Saxon origin with parts of the existing building dating from the Norman period.

A road from near the church runs north past Peldon Lodge; it is now a no-through road that stops at the edge of the reservoir. At one time it continued to Butler's Farm and on towards Colchester. Although the reservoir covered many acres of productive farmland very few people were displaced. Butler's Farm along with Layer House, each partly in the parish of Peldon, were the only dwellings to be demolished before the valley was flooded.

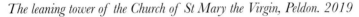

The leaning tower of the Church of St Mary the Virgin, Peldon. 2019

View from the bird hide at the end of the path that was the road, which at one time continued across the valley now filled by the reservoir.

The parish that lost the most land to the reservoir was Layer-de-la-Haye. This parish is centred on the high ground between Layer Brook and Roman River and extends to each. I will leave a more detailed description of some features of this parish until I continue my way up the Roman River Valley. The other two parishes that take part of their name from the brook are Layer Breton and Layer Marney, which is where I am heading next.

Only three buildings were lost below the reservoir; Layer House, Butler's and Billett's.

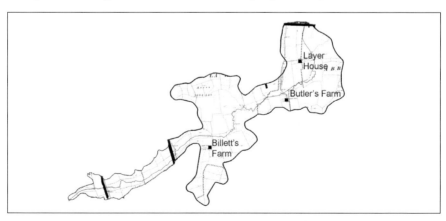

CHAPTER 5 iii

Layer Breton

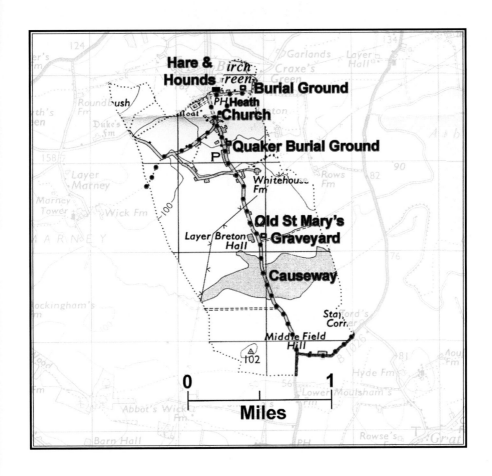

At the top the Church with trees and geese representing the Heath plus fish for the reservoir and other wildlife. The arms are those of St Catherine's College and St John's Abbey both landowners in earlier times. Barley and wheat depict the farming interest and the whole surrounds the arms of the Norman le Breton family from which the village is named.

The parish name consists of two parts; Layer from the river and Breton, the name of the family who were lords of the manor from Norman times until the 15th century.

In the Domesday Book of 1086 the whole of Layer, which later became Layer Breton, Layer-de-la-Haye and Layer Marney was recorded as a single entity of nine entries. This was a large area in which no less than five mills were recorded, some of which would have been on the Roman River.

In 1848 White described Layer Breton as a village and parish in the vale of a rivulet with 290 inhabitants and 965 acres of land, including 37 acres of heath. The Briton, or Breton family, who came with the Conqueror, had lands here.

The population of the parish of Layer Breton in 2011 was 287.

The parish is named after the Breton family who were lords of the manor for several hundred years following the Norman Conquest. It has the honour of having one of the reservoir causeways named after it but only a small part of the parish lies to the south of the reservoir. The road to the north of the causeway passes Layer Breton Hall, a fine 18th century red-brick house. Opposite, on the other side of the road, is the site of the former parish church of St Mary. Nothing remains of the church but a few stones in the graveyard. Just behind the site of this former church is a complete mediaeval, rectangular moat that is very likely the site of an earlier hall. The church was demolished in 1915 having been weakened and rendered unstable by the 1884 earthquake.

A watercolour painted in 1909 by Thomas Simpson, sometime Churchwarden of layer Breton Church. The church, with its wooden bell turret containing one bell was said to be of ancient origin and contained a monument to Alice, wife of Nicholas Breton who died in 1392. It stood opposite Layer Breton Hall and was demolished in 1915 as unsafe.

The road continues past the Hall before rising steeply into the centre of the village, which is marked with the village sign. Behind this is the site of the former Quaker Meeting House, demolished in 1988 to make way for new houses, although the burial ground remains. A little further on at the edge of the heath stands the new church of St Mary the Virgin. This was built on a site closer to village population to replace the demolished one at the bottom of the hill. WWI caused a delay in the construction of the building, which was not completed until 1922.

On the other side of the heath was a Congregational Chapel, founded in 1798. The congregation grew for many years, as did that of the Quaker Meeting House, which opened in 1827. It has been suggested that the community needed so many churches because they

St Mary's graveyard. 2019

St Mary the Virgin, Layer Breton, built in 1922 to replace the earlier church at the bottom of the hill, which was demolished in 1915.

were so godless. Be that as it may, the Congregational Chapel is no longer but its burial ground remains and the substantial, adjoining schoolroom has been put to a number of uses over the years and is now a private residence.

Chapman & Andre's 1777 map of Essex shows Colchester encircled with heaths. This is no longer the case as enclosures, the expansion of urban areas and the changing patterns of animal husbandry have all contributed to the loss of heaths. The continuing survival of Layer Breton Heath, one of the few remaining heathland sites in Essex, now depends upon active management.

Since the fire of 1976 livestock no longer graze the area. This has led to considerable areas of the Heath being taken over by birch

Birch, Layer Breton & Layer Marney Local History

*The Chapel, with the minister's house (The Manse) on the right and
to the left the Sunday School, now Breton House. On the far left Heathcote,
the* Hare & Hounds *and Heath House are visible.*

and oak trees. These have provided shade and leaf-mould which has
increased the fertility of the soil, which in turn has facilitated the growth
of stronger plants that have out-competed the specialised heathland
species that formerly flourished in the poor soil. The heath now has
many more diverse habitats which all need active management to
ensure their survival. This management can only be successful with
the cooperation of the increasing numbers of local residents and
visitors and dog walkers who all affect the heathland environment by
the manner in which they use it.

Contrary to popular belief, common land is not public land. Most
commons are privately owned but commoners have a right to use
the land for specific purposes; and not all commoners have the same
rights. As far as Layer Breton Heath is concerned, the Lord of the
Manor owns it. Ancient rights entitle everyone to a right of access for
the purposes of air and exercise, or to ride a horse across it. Certain
owners of property in the village have additional rights, for example, to
graze a number of geese or cattle on the heath. More recent legislation

Layer Breton Congregational Burial Ground in a quiet corner of the heath. 2019

concerning nature conservation and the protection of particular wildlife habitats has placed obligations on both authorities and users. For several years the Layer Breton Heath Management Committee managed all these disparate aspects of the heath. It is now under a conservation programme funded by Natural England as a ten year Countryside Stewardship Agreement with the Lord of the Manor, this

Layer Breton Quaker Burial Ground hidden away behind a row of houses built since 1988 when the Meeting House was demolished. 2019

programme is being carried out by Essex Wildlife Trust. All this relies on the cooperation of all the various interest groups to maintain the very special nature of the heath for the benefit of all.

Before leaving the heath I paid a visit to the *Hare and Hounds*. This is on the edge of the heath. According to the locals the hostelry straddles the parish boundary between Layer Breton and Birch, which meant that I was still in Layer Breton but was being served by the publican on the other side of the bar in Birch.

Refreshed by my pint and sandwich I left the pub, crossed the road, crossed a few yards of greensward and then another road. This second road came into existence along with the Congregational Chapel to enable the villagers to access their place of worship without having to endure the temptation of passing the pub door! The chapel is long gone only the road and the pub remain. I crossed the heath to Shatters Road, which leads to the neighbouring parish of Layer Marney. Soon after leaving the heath the striking outline of Layer Marney Tower appeared on the skyline. At a bend the road veers from the direct route but an ancient footpath continues straight on towards the tower.

The Hare & Hounds *on the edge of the heath straddles the border between Layer Breton and Birch. 2019*

CHAPTER 5 iv

Layer Marney

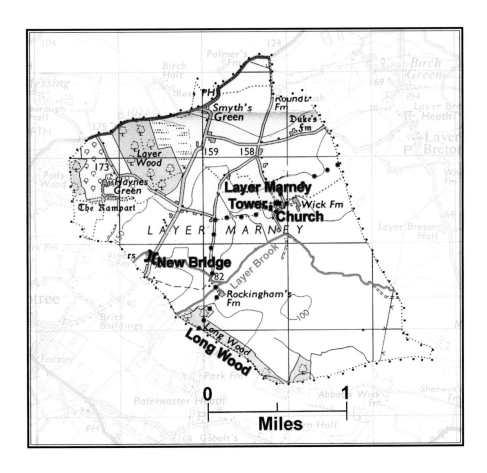

Dominant is the Tower along with St Mary's Church. The sign shows a tractor, a turkey and a Friesian cow, also a rhea's egg, a bird that has been bred in the parish. The central arms are of St Mary the Virgin. The arms of the Marney family appear on the other side of the sign.

The parish name consists of two parts; Layer from the river and Marney, the name of the family who were lords of the manor from the 12th century.

As mentioned earlier, in the Domesday Book of 1086 the whole of Layer was recorded as a single entity.

In 1848 White described Layer Marney as a scattered parish of 256 inhabitants.

The population of the parish of Layer Marney in 2011 was 199.

Layer Marney is a farming parish without any real centre. There are various clusters of houses but the population is too small to sustain any organised community life.

Layer Brook makes a small contribution to the waters of the reservoir as it enters its western end by tumbling over a weir at the eastern extremity of the parish. This is less than a mile below Layer Marney Tower with associated Hall Farm and St Mary's Church.

The ancient Norman church of St Mary the Virgin was rebuilt by the 1st Lord Marney at the beginning of the 16th century. It is built in the perpendicular style of locally made Tudor brick and contains the impressive tombs of the 1st Lord Marney who died in 1523, and his son John, the 2nd Lord Marney.

The church of St Mary the Virgin, Layer Marney. 2019

Alongside the church stands the gatehouse and an array of outbuildings set in gardens and parkland which, in totality, could be described as a Tudor palace. The Marneys have a long lineage; they had held the manor, which has taken their name and many neighbouring estates, since the 12th century. But the man who is most remembered is Henry, the 1st Lord Marney, a man of exceptional ability who became a trusted advisor to the Tudor monarchs Henry VII and his successor Henry VIII, who rewarded him for his services as Privy Councillor by raising him to the peerage as Lord Marney.

The tomb of Henry Lord Marney 1457-1523. This is unusual in that it is thought to depict his actual likeness. 2019

Lord Marney planned to build a much larger house, with three additional wings to enclose a grand central courtyard, but he died before it was finished. His son continued the enterprise but he too died but two years later. Their achievement is the tower, which remains the tallest and finest Tudor gatehouse in the country. It overlooks the diminutive Layer Brook and the more distant Blackwater estuary.

I continued along the footpath and then down the lane to Rockingham's Farm where Layer Brook is joined by a tributary. This rises in the west of the parish at Haynes Green and is fed by several springs before flowing under Newbridge Road. A short distance from

Layer Marney Towers. 2019

The rather inconspicuous Newbridge, that crosses a tributary of Layer Brook at the bottom of Newbridge Road. 2019

Beneath the leveled surface of the road is the brick arch structure that would, originally, have been a hump-back bridge with brick parapets, the copping stones of which are now reused as kerbs to the road. 2019

the bridge is the Old Bakery. When this was established in 1851 its water supply was pumped up from the brook. At this time the parish was still responsible for the upkeep of the roads and bridges. The records of the maintenance of Newbridge are sparse; the earliest one I have found is from 1629, which makes it not such a new bridge after all.

Back at Rockingham's Farm the road comes to an end but a footpath continues up the hill into Long Wood. In the wood the path continues to ascend until it leaves the wood where I was confronted with a ploughed field. My map shows the path continuing straight on and I see a few sticky footprints pointing in the direction of Park Farm. The parish boundary runs along the edge of the wood, so I will delay the description of my progress across the field until the next parish of Tolleshunt Knights.

The footpath from Rockingham's Farm leading into Long Wood. 2019.

CHAPTER 5 v

Tolleshunt Knights

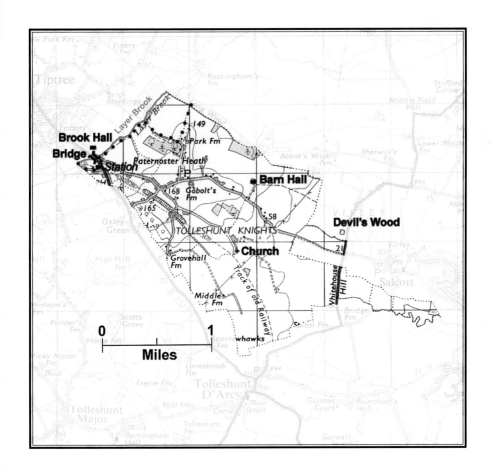

Tolleshunt Knights does not have a village sign.

The parish name consists of two parts; is thought to be derived from the Saxon, Tolle who controlled the large area that became Tolleshunt, which is derived from Tolle's springs. During the 13th century part of this area was held by William le Chivaler. Chivalers is the Norman-French for Knights, this name has been attached to the parish ever since.

In the Domesday Book of 1086 the whole of Tolleshunt, which later became Tolleshunt Major, Tolleshunt D'Arcy and Tolleshunt Knights. This was a large area of four manors.

In 1848 White described Tolleshunt Knights as a parish of scattered houses mostly on high ground. It includes part of Tiptree Heath, and contains 313 souls, and 1921 acres of land, in two manors. The soil is chiefly a tenacious red clay and partly a gravelly loam.

The population of the parish of Tolleshunt Knights in 2011 was 1030.

I trudged across the field, my boots getting heavier with each step as they picked up more and more of the glutinous clay. After crossing two ploughed fields the path followed the field-edge of the third where the plough had left just enough headland for walkers to create their own less glutinous, darker brown glaur to squelch though.

At Park Farm I joined Park Lane. This is a narrow, hedged bridleway, an ancient highway, which connects the two villages of Tolleshunt Knights and Tiptree. I walked along here in a westerly direction until I reached Layer Brook and a footpath that followed its bank.

For the first time since leaving Abberton I walked beside the brook. The path was obviously well used by the local dog walkers who had created a mud of yet another consistency, a less sticky but splashier mixture, to slip and slide through. Fortunately it was not far to the

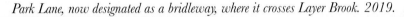

Park Lane, now designated as a bridleway, where it crosses Layer Brook. 2019.

The footpath alongside Layer Brook that now forms the boundary between Tolleshunt Knights and the new civil parish of Tiptree. 2019

*Brook Hall with Layer Brook in the foreground. The original site of the
Hall was closer to the brook. 2019*

cross paths from where, unlike the majority, I continued alongside the brook. Soon Brook Hall came into view and the path wound its way between the high-fenced gardens of the properties alongside Brook Road, which becomes Factory Hill once it has crossed Layer Brook. Just over the bridge stands Brook Hall, a fine Georgian building. This replaced the old manor house that stood closer to the brook. It was one of the four manors, which were recorded in the Domesday Book, that for many years made up the parish of Tolleshunt Knights. The only other hall in the parish to stand on relatively high ground is Barn Hall and legend has it that its elevated site was chosen by the Devil.

Like all legends, its origins are lost in the mists of time. One of the earliest written accounts of the story appeared in the 1820 edition of *The Gentleman's Magazine*. This was based on what the writer had heard

The bridge over Layer Brook where the B1023 changes its name from Brook Road to Factory Hill. 2019.

as a child when he visited the area in 1761. Since then there have been several further publications, all slightly different, but obviously an interpretation of the same legend.

One version of the story goes something like this. Low down on a piece of land near the parish boundary stood a wood; a wood to which the Devil laid claim. Ignoring superstition, some say this was chosen by a knight as the site to build Barn Hall. The work proceeded and was guarded each night by the fearless knight with his dogs. All went well until one night Satan visited the wood and asked, 'Who is there?' The knight replied, 'God and myself and my spey bitches.' On hearing this Satan retreated. The following night Satan returned with the same question and received the same reply, 'God and myself and my spey bitches.' And again Satan retreated. On the third night Satan returned

Brook Hall, this fine Georgian building replaced the old manor house in the late 18th century. 2019.

yet again and repeated his question. This time the knight replied a little carelessly, 'myself and my spey bitches, and God. The mistake of putting himself before God cost him his life as Satan tore out his heart and screamed that he would have his soul whether he was buried in church or churchyard. In his rage he destroyed the partially built

Barn Hall and farm as it appeared in 1921

hall and tossed a beam high above the trees and up the hill shouting, 'Where this beam lands, is where Barn Hall will be built.'

The beam is reputed to be in the cellar of Barn Hall, now part of Barn Hall Farm, and it is said it bears the marks of the Devil's claws and cannot be cut or damaged by anyone without injuring themselves.

Devil's Wood, formerly part of Barn Hall lands, is now a small, solitary area of woodland surrounded by acres of arable fields in the neighbouring parish of Virley where traces of a moat and the foundation of a building are still identifiable.

The former parish church of All Saints' contains an effigy of a knight which some say is that of Sir John Atte Lee who died in 1370 and one time lord of the manor. Some versions of the legend link this knight to the aforementioned Barn Hall story. Supporters of this

*All Saints'
Church,
Tolleshunt
Knights. Parts
of the rubble
walls date
back to the 12th
century with a
later porch and
a timber belfry
with 2 bells and
a shingled spire.
~1950*

*All Saints'
Church,
Tolleshunt
Knights, which
was sold by
the Church of
England to the
Greek Orthodox
Church in 1958
who now use
it as a chapel.
2019*

The effigy of the knight in All Saints' Church, Tolleshunt Knights. In 1761 it was described as a very ancient monument of soft stone, a full-length effigy of a knight in armour and helmet, two dogs at his feet. By 1922 it was listed in the Royal Commission of Ancient Monuments as a mutilated effigy of a man in armour with basinet and hands holding a heart, arms and legs broken off.

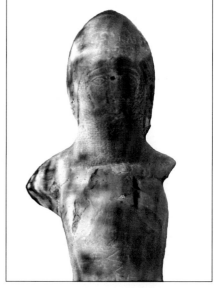

Part of the effigy has survived and is still recognizable as that of a Knight but it has lost its dogs, legs, arms and heart. It appears to be considerably more weathered. Maybe there is still lingering suspicion as it is now kept behind a grill in a niche within the Church wall, neither 'in church or churchyard'. 2019

idea claim there are several aspects of the much-mutilated effigy that support their claim. The most significant of which was that it was found in the walls of the church, neither in nor out. Has he thwarted the Devil's claim on his soul?

In 1958 the Church of England sold the church to the Greek Orthodox Church who use it as a chapel attached to the Monastery of St John the Baptist, which they established in grounds around the Old Rectory. I first visited the Monastery in the late 1960s, since then the community has grown to around forty, both men and women. It is an oasis of peace and tranquility.

Close by the church are the remains of a long gone railway. One of the first to moot the idea of a railway through Tolleshunt Knights was another lord of the manor of Barn Hall. In 1895 he donated five acres of land for the project and then, during the following year, the Light Railway Act was passed which provided a government subsidy. Other landowners donated land that allowed construction to begin in 1902. Two years later saw the opening the line between Kelvedon and Tollesbury, with intermediate stations at Feering, Inworth, Tiptree, Tolleshunt Knights and Tolleshunt d'Arcy.

Work continued on the extension to Tollesbury pier, which was opened 2½ years later. There were grand plans to develop the land around the pier as a yachting resort with the pier providing access to continental packet steamers. WWI put pay to these dreams and the line to the pier was closed to passengers in 1921.

By 1948 which saw the creation of the nationlised British Railways, passenger numbers on the line were negligible and there was little opposition to its closure in 1951. However the section from Kelvedon to Tiptree was kept open for freight until 1962. The principle user of this section was Wilkins whose factory is situated at Trewlands at the top of Factory Hill. This, like Brook Hall, was originally in the parish of Tolleshunt Knights, but their conserves have carried the name Tiptree from the beginning, long before the parish of Tiptree was formed in 1934.

Tolleshunt Knights Station consisted of a name-board, two oil lamp standards and a waiting room converted from an old coach body. It stood by the level crossing in D'Arcy Road. No trace of the station or rail bed remain today.

CHAPTER 5 vi

Tiptree

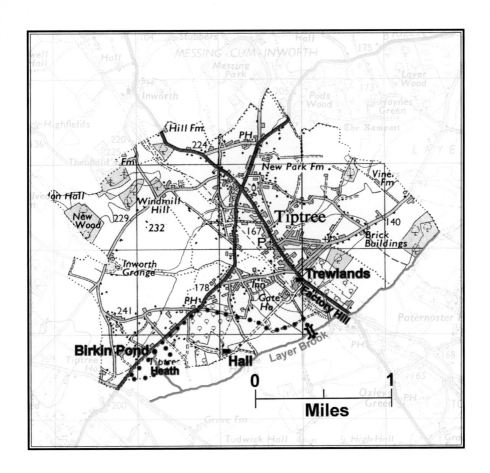

The Tiptree sign is of the colour green which is the corporate colour of Wilkin & Sons Ltd, who export their fruit preserves, particularly strawberry, and the name Tiptree the world over.

The parish name is thought to be named after a Saxon named Tippa who controlled a considerable area including what became Tiptree Heath which has been recorded in several variations of Tippetre, which is thought to be derived from Tippa's tree.

The Parish of Tiptree was not created until 1934, mostly from parts of the surrounding ancient parishes of Inworth, Messing and Tolleshunt Knights.

In the Domesday Book the area is recorded merely as unnamed 'woodland for swine'. Some sixteen neighbouring villages enjoyed common of pasture over its wilds, but the soil was owned by various lords of manors, who were responsible for its preservation or enclosure,

In 1848 the entry in White's Gazetteer describes Tiptree Heath as extending into many parishes. It includes an unenclosed area of about 500 acres, reduced from some 1000 acres 50 years ago.

The population of the parish of Tiptree in 2011 was 9,182.

It is thought that the name Tiptree is derived from the name of a Saxon leader called Tippa. The area associated with this person has been variously recorded as Typpetre, Tipentrie, Tippetre, Typettre, Typetre, Tiptre Heth and Tiptree Comon. The version *Typpetre* appears in a charter of 1225 and has been interpreted as Tippa's tree, and refers to the area of land that eventually became Tiptree Heath that covered several thousand acres. This was described by G W Johnson in 1831 as, 'a wild district, on which, in the memory of man but few houses occurred between Heybridge and Colchester, a distance of fifteen miles. With an inclination to the east, and varied with stagnant waters, whose evaporation tended constantly to reduce the temperature, this district became the proverbial illustration of desolation and "Cold Tiptree Heath" was considered the abode of disease and wretchedness - ague and poverty.'

Shortly after this was written a man arrived in the area who was about to change all that. This was John Mechi, the son of an Italian immigrant. He was a polymath; a man who succeeded in many enterprises. He was a silversmith, banker, inventor and Alderman of the City of London. Two of his most successful inventions were 'Mechi's Magic Razor' and his patented razor strop; it was these that generated his fortune, which enabled him to buy one of the impoverished farms on the heath.

John Mechi bought the farm along with its unremarkable farmhouse built of lath and plaster, then called Sadlers, in 1841. He demolished the house and replaced it with a modest mansion which he renamed Tiptree Hall. He regarded the unproductive farm as a challenge and set about developing pioneering methods that transformed the poor marshy land into a model farm. Here he pioneered deep drainage and the application of liquid manure using a system of pipes powered by a steam engine. The farm became a model farm that was visited by people from all over the country. His book, *How to Farm Profitably* was popular when first

A page from Mechi's catalogue.

published in 1857 and ran to several editions.

Coupled with John Mechi's new ideas in farm improvement, he was active in the improvement of the district in general. It is said he was the initiator of the group that led to the establishment of the ecclesiastical parish of Tiptree Heath and the opening of the new church of St Luke's in 1858. He was also acutely aware of the poverty and hardship suffered by many in the farming community. In an effort to ameliorate this, he founded what was to become the Royal Agricultural Benevolent Institution.

Somewhat ironically, despite his selfless dedication to the improvement of farming methods and the welfare of the workers, he was not immune to the combined effects of a succession of poor harvests, ill-health and bad investments. He died virtually bankrupt, but his legacy lives on.

*Tiptree Hall, built in 1843
by John Mechi.*

John Joseph Mechi 1802-1880.

If it had not been for Mechi it is doubtful that the neighboring farm, Trewlands would have become so productive and lead to the creation of Wilkin & Sons Ltd., a name now synonymous with Tiptree. Arthur Charles Wilkin produced the first 'conserve' from fruit grown on the farm in 1885. Since then Trewlands has become the site of the factory and the company has acquired several neighbouring farms, as well as some further afield. Tiptree Hall is now the residence of Peter John Wilkin, the chairman and great grandson of the founder. The company is now the principle employer in the village and has an international customer base with a multi-million pound turnover.

Part of John Mechi's original farm included a small piece of land that is still called Tiptree Heath. This area was never subject to Mechi's improvement schemes and is now owned by the present occupant of the hall, Peter Wilkin. The area is registered as a common and although there are no public rights of way on Tiptree Heath, there

Wilkin & Sons Ltd and the original Trewlands farmhouse. 2019

is open access throughout the area although people generally keep to the paths and open areas. It is managed jointly by the Friends of Tiptree Heath and Essex Wildlife Trust. The 61-acre heath is the largest surviving fragment of heathland in Essex and is a Site of Special Scientific Interest. Historically the area was a focal point for smugglers, who brought their contraband from the secluded inlets of the Blackwater Estuary up to the heath to trade or hide it in the overgrown heathland.

Something else that is hidden within the heath is the source of Layer Brook. There are two ponds on the heath; the one near the car park is known as the Birkin Pond. For many years this was used by cattle owned by the Birkin family who lived across the road at Manor House Farm. The pond is fed by small springs on this farm whose waters accumulate in the pond and overflow into a recognizable stream that flows across the heath. This stream joins several others that flow through the Wilkin farmland that form the headwaters of Layer Brook.

Birkin Pond on Tiptree Heath. 2019.

Public access to the brook headwater is limited but there is a footpath that runs between Tiptree Hall Lane and Tudwick Lane. This crosses the brook close to a Wilkin reservoir, which is filled with water pumped from the brook.

Having explored Layer Brook to its source I will return to Roman River to take up my story from where I left it in the parish of Layer-de-la-Haye.

From Birkin pond a stream flows across Tiptree Heath. This is one of the headwater streams of Layer Brook. 2019.

CHAPTER 6

Layer-de-la-Haye

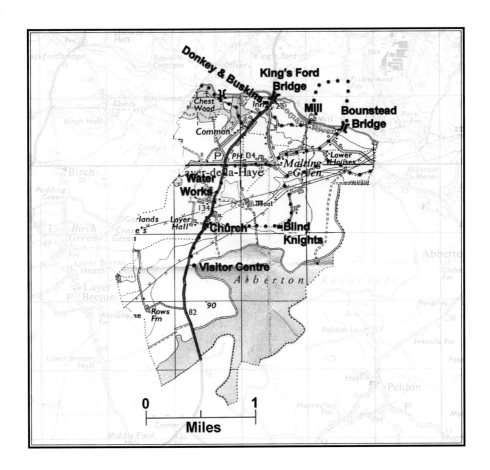

The central feature of this sign is the crest of the de la Haye family. This is flanked by St John- the-Baptist Church which overlooks the reservoir, and the old forge at the crossroads. Below the village name are images of pike, cormorant and wavy lines all representing the reservoir.

The parish name consists of two parts; Layer is thought to be derived from the Celtic word leir for the marshy clay ground associated with the valley, after the Conquest two of the manors were controlled by the De la Haye family who came from Normandy.

As mentioned earlier, in the Domesday Book of 1086 the whole of Layer was recorded as a single entity.

In 1848 White described Layer-de-la-Hay as a pleasant village on a commanding eminence, overlooking the small river Roman and one of its tributary streams.

The population of the parish of Layer-de-la-Haye in 2011 was 1767.

I am now going back to Roman River to follow it up from its confluence with Layer Brook, which is where the parishes of Abberton, Berechurch and Layer-de-la-Haye meet.

The parish of Layer-de-la-Haye occupies the ridge of land between the two rivers, Birch Brook and Roman River. Part of the earlier parish is now submerged below the waters of the reservoir whose dam now forms part of its modified boundary. Since the reservoir was enlarged in 2015 permissive paths around it now link public footpaths from Peldon Lodge to Layer-de-la-Haye Church via Abberton Church. I will start

A warning sign for those using the permissive path that crosses Layer Brook below Abberton Reservoir dam. (2019)

Abberton Reservoir Wild Birds Sanctuary Order. (2019)

my exploration where this path enters the parish as it crosses Layer Brook below the dam.

The path soon joins the lane that leads to Blind Knights. This ancient site now overlooks the reservoir. Parts of the building date back to the early 14th century when it was used as a hospice for Knights Templar who were blinded or injured in the Crusades.

The path continues across open country with pleasant views over the reservoir before passing through fields of grazing sheep and entering St John the Baptist's churchyard. There has been a church in this commanding position since Norman times. The extensive views from

Blind Knights, Layer-de-la-Haye. 2019

its 14th century tower, of the reservoir and as far afield as Bradwell and Clacton, are impressive.

The path continues around the reservoir to the Essex Wildlife Trust Visitor Centre where there is a café, extensive facilities for bird watchers and information about the many and varied activities the Trust provides.

From here I retraced my route back to the church of St John the Baptist and continued past the water treatment works. This is where the water from the reservoir is cleaned and purified before entering the drinking water distribution network. At the crossroads a 17th century building is where the *Fox Inn* moved to in 1839.

From here I proceeded along Malting Green Road and Abberton Road to Bounstead Hill, which took me down to Bounstead Bridge

Abberton Reservoir from the tower of St John the Baptist's Church, Layer-de-la-Haye. 2018

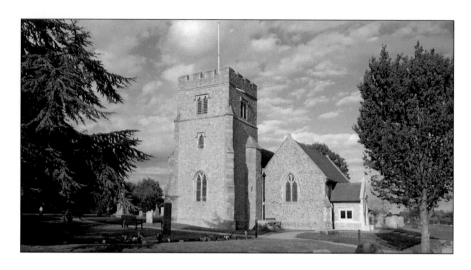

The Church of St John the Baptist, Layer-de-la-Haye. First recorded in 1128. The nave and tower were rebuilt after the Black Death and date from about 1350. The tower houses a mediaeval bellframe, which for many years contained five bells. Following the 1884 earthquake they could not be rung until a grant from the Millennium fund facilitated the completion of a restoration project that included an additional bell. In 2001 the first Quarter Peal using six bells rang out. 2019

over Roman River. This has been referred to as Brounsford, Bouncers and Bounsted Bridge. This was as far as my earlier walk had taken me along this river.

Brounsford Bridge was first recorded in 1563. The bridge that existed in 1846 was known as Bounstead Bridge but this fell down in 1876. From then on the river was forded until a footbridge was erected in the late 19th century, followed by a new bridge built by Mrs Hetherington of Berechurch Hall in 1911. This has since been replaced by a flat concrete and steel girder structure.

There is no riverside path upstream from here. To continue my journey along Roman River I must leave the parish to travel the half-

The opening of the new Bounstead Bridge in 1911

Bounstead Road Bridge looking north with Friday wood on the right. 2019

The Steel girder and concrete construction of Bounstead Road Bridge. 2019

mile or so upstream to Layer-de-la-Haye Mill. First climb the hill towards Fridaywood Farm then, just before I reach the farm, I take the footpath that crosses fields of grazing sheep and sometimes of soldiers on manoeuvres. The field is bounded by a line of ancient oaks, which mark the course of another public footpath. I turn to the left and follow, what was once a tree-lined lane that descends back down to the river and the site of Layer-de-la-Haye Mill. The lane had fallen into disuse by the early 19th century when the mill was described, as 'A desolate place with no-through road, and the lane was a mere track across the surrounding heath.'

The original mill on this site was built by Eustace, Earl of Boulogne shortly after the Norman Conquest. It was the only place his tenants were allowed to grind their corn and he charged them for the service. Later it was owned by John de Rye who donated the mill, along with

The late 18th century, weather-boarded Layer-de-la-Haye Mill. 2019

his land, to St John's Abbey in Colchester.

After the dissolution of the monasteries by Henry VIII, Sir Thomas Audley of Berechurch Hall appropriated both the land and the mill. The 19th century millers were Dan Cooper followed by John Royce then William Royce for 44 years and finally Joseph Norfolk. The mill ended its working life grinding a product used in the cultivation of mushrooms. In 1960 the wheel and machinery were stripped out and the building converted into a house. Today the mill retains the character of a modest country mill, complete with lucum. The surviving external iron wheel was probably belt-driven by a portable steam or diesel unit when the water was low.

It is here that my walk takes me back into the parish of Layer-de-la-Haye. The path proceeds along the valley beside field edges and through lightly wooded areas to emerge into The Folley near

Layer millrace, a surprisingly powerful flow for what often appears a sluggish, river. 2019

the *Donkey & Buskins*. This welcoming free-house now offers a good selection of food and drink as well as accommodation; a far cry from when it opened as a beer house back in the 1850s. Its unique name is said to have arisen from the story that one of its former landlords kept donkeys on the adjoining heath. He wrapped sacking around their legs to protect them from the gorse; and this made them look as if they were wearing buskins, an alternative name for puttees, gaiters or spats.

This hostelry stands atop the steep hill that drops down into the Roman River Valley at Kingsford Bridge. If this bridge had ever been crossed by enemy troops during WWII they would have been confronted by a spigot mortar installed opposite the pub, in a good defensive position to attack them as they advanced up the hill. Many spigot mortars were manufactured in 1941 to replace the anti-tank weapons lost after the evacuation of the Army at Dunkirk. Thousands were made but the Army refused to use them because they could only be used at short range, and when they exploded

The buildings that were once used for mushroom cultivation. 2019

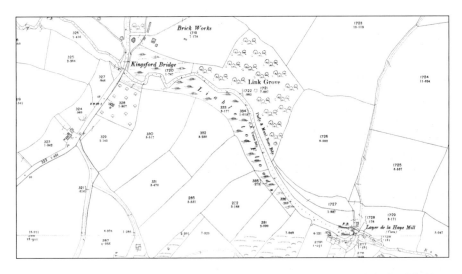

The 1ˢᵗ edition OS map of 1862 shows the extent of the millpond and the land liable to flood upstream of Layer-de-la-Haye Mill.

Layer-de-la-Haye Mill sluice still holds back the water in the millpond that drove the millwheel in earlier times. 2019

119

The Donkey & Buskins *with a Landau outside. ~1900*

A loaded spigot mortar on a mount similar to that at Layer-de-la-Haye ready for use. c1942

The Donkey & Buskins *with the WWII spigot mortar mounting pin in the bottom right hand corner. 2019*

fragments were often projected back at the firing crew. Never the less, they were issued to the Home Guard. No doubt the local unit would have practiced mounting the weapon on its pin in the centre of its concrete block which, at that time, would have been in a concrete pit with ammunition alcoves. These may still remain beneath the earth around the pedestal. It is fortunate that these weapons never had to be used as their limited range meant that the target would need to be close to the pub before it was fired, and on impact it is likely the explosion would have projected debris back into those who had fired it. A little further along the valley we will see how the defensive properties of the valley were probably used more effectively by our forebears some two millennia earlier.

After a pint and a sandwich in the *Donkey & Buskins*, I walked down the hill to Kingsford Bridge. Not a comfortable walk on a busy road with no footpath. Most folk drive along this stretch of road so fast that they are unaware there is a bridge at all. There is a record of a bridge here as early as 1392 but the present single-arch brick structure was built by Essex County Council in 1892. A time when people still had time to notice the dated plaque in the bridge parapet. The bricks could well have been made at the brickfield adjacent to the bridge.

The Essex Wildlife Trust manages the river upstream from the bridge, along with a strip of land on the north bank, and a much narrower strip on the south. Maps from the 19th century show field boundaries running down as far as this strip which at that time was probably meadow. The land either side of this strip rises sharply and on the Layer-de-la-Haye side is owned by the Colchester Rifle Club (CRC). Their land extends from the road upstream as far as a right angle bend in the river. It looks as if the river could have continued straight on in earlier times and still does when it floods. There are traces of this former riverbed running through as far as the bridge. When I have visited this site in winter there is often water in one

The brick built single arch Kingsford Bridge. 2018

Layer Road as it crosses Kingsford Bridge. 2018

Essex County Council 1892 plaque on the western parapet of Kingsford Bridge. 2018

section near the bridge, forming a small oxbow lake. There have been considerable changes made to the profile of the valley here. Beneath the thin layer of topsoil of the higher land a considerable quantity of sand and gravel was excavated for the construction of the nearby WWII airfield at Birch. The present uneven terrain shows the remnants of the naturalised remains of these pits and spoil heaps. Subsequently, during the post war period, parts of the side of the valley were levelled at ascending heights during the construction of the CRC ranges. The surrounding safety area is managed by the club as a nature reserve. This adjoins the public accessible area of Chest Wood, which can be reached from the *Donkey & Buskins* by walking up the hill and taking the footpath from New Cut.

Chest Wood is the name given to the area of woodland that extends from the High Road residential area to the parish boundary with Birch to the west and Roman River to the north. Chest Wood is the name often given to the whole area that includes the smaller adjoining woodland areas of Charity Wood, Heather Fields and Needles Eye Wood. Its undulating terrain is criss-crossed by numerous paths. There is a footbridge across Roman River that takes a path up the other side of the valley into Oliver's Copse.

I continued through Chest Wood to a second more substantial bridge that is accompanied by a ford. This is the crossing place of Leas Lane, an ancient thoroughfare that is officially designated as a bridleway and is also part of the Sustrans National Cycleway Network Route 1.

Sustrans is an organisation, created in 1977, with the aim of promoting sustainable transport by cycling and walking. The first project was to convert a disused railway line between Bristol and Bath into a route for cycling and walking. The success of this project sparked a cycling and walking revolution with the development of many more new routes in various parts of the UK. By 1995 there were

*The footbridge across Roman River on the path between Chest Wood
and Olivers Copse. 2019*

enough for the creation of a national network. Work started on this
ambitious project with the help of National Lottery funding, hundreds
of partners and thousands volunteers and numerous supporters. The
success of this ongoing project and the organisation's campaigning
resulted, in 2012, Wales becoming the first country to place a legal
duty on councils to provide a network of routes for walking and
cycling; and, in 2017, Scotland to double its 'active travel' budget.
With the support of its many members and over 3,500 volunteers
Sustrans now sustains a network used for nearly 800 million journeys
a year. There are over 16,000 miles of route of which over 5,000 are
designated as traffic-free.

Part of Leas Lane is part of this network that is now designated as
National Cycle Route 1. This is a long-distance route of 1,695 miles

Leas Lane Ford, below Oliver's. 2019

from Dover to the Shetland Isles.

This is an extremely varied route that takes the traveller to many of the UK's cultural and natural highlights. From the White Cliffs of Dover to London; from Edinburgh to the wild mountain scenery of Scotland, and the attractions of Canterbury, Colchester, Sutton Hoo, Norfolk Broads, Whitby along with many others and all the charms of the less well known.

Over the bridge is Stanway, but for now, I will stay south of the river to explore the adjoining parish of Birch.

National Cycle Route 1 as it crosses Leas Lane Bridge, below Oliver's. 2019

CHAPTER 7

Birch

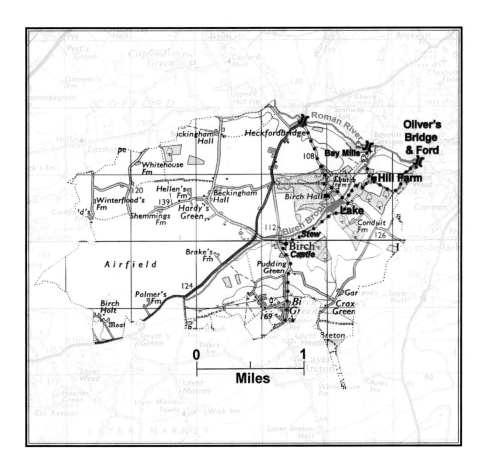

Surrounding the coat of arms of the Round family are the arms of St Peter and St Mary representing the two churches. There are also shields of two other families with local connections, the Gernon family held land in Norman times and the Tendring family were patrons of the living from the 14th to the 18th centuries. The sign is surmounted by an ancient castle representing the fact that Birch had a motte and bailey castle in much earlier times. Local wild life is reflected in a pheasant and a fish.

It would be understandable to assume the parish name, Birch, has something to do with the tree of the same name. However, place name experts have delved into the past and discovered the early spelling of the place was Brich which is thought to be derived from the Old English bryce. This means breaking in the sense of creating cultivated land from woodland clearings

Recorded in the Domesday Book in 1086 as Great and Little Birch. Great Birch was in the hands of Robert Gernon, It contained one mill.

In 1848 White described Birch (Great and Little) as a straggling village of 794 souls and 3009 acres. An artificial mound, near the church, is said to be the site of Birch Castle.

The population of the parish of Birch in 2011 was 873

I often take a rest on the bench by Leas Lane Bridge just because I find it a pleasant place to be. It is an ancient crossing place; carts no longer use the ford but horses cross by the bridge and sometimes drink from the ford. Many more may like to, as like me they know every way from here is up.

Leas Lane follows the parish boundary of the former Little Birch. This and the neighbouring Great Birch have been regarded as a single parish for several centuries. An Act of Parliament and the modern civil parish of Birch give this fact official recognition. At the top of the hill Leas Lane turns away from Chest Wood and the track proceeds along the valley side to Hill Farm. This is where the lane divides, one way leads back down to Roman River, the other to its tributary, Birch Brook. It is a junction I will return to later. Meanwhile I turn to my left to begin my exploration of Birch Brook, the second significant

Hill Farm barn. 2019

The weir below Birch Hall Lake. 2019

Birch Hall Lake. 2019

*The ruined 12ᵗʰ century nave and 16ᵗʰ century brick tower of St Mary's church,
Little Birch. 2019*

tributary of Roman River. This flows in a steep-sided valley, which I
soon descend into. I follow the footpath, which is in fact a track, that
leads from Hill Farm to the road that crosses Birch Brook Valley on the
top of the dam built to create Birch Hall Lake.

A short way along this road are the ruins of St Mary's Church, the
long disused church of Little Birch. Records indicate the church was
in regular use in the pre-Reformation years when the Tendring and
Forster families lived at the nearby hall. It appears to have fallen into
disuse soon after the Reformation and by 1709 was reported to have
been in a ruinous state. In 1768 Philip Morant describes the church
as 'ruinous, the tower which is pretty high and the walls only being
standing, but the roof is quite gone.'

Meanwhile, in 1724, Little Birch Hall was purchased by James
Round whose family rebuilt the Hall and enlarged the estate to include

The Georgian Birch Hall built by James Round as it appeared in 1772.

The large and dignified Italianate villa built by Charles Gray Round in 1843-7 to replace the smaller but attractive 18th century Georgian house.

large parts of Great Birch, whose parish church of St Peter & St Paul became the one used by both parishes for normal services as well as the burial place of members of the Round Family. In 1816 an Act of

The refurbished Birch Hall. 2019

Parliament united the two parishes and the site of Little Birch Church became the property of the hall by which time this was known simply as Birch Hall.

The attractive Georgian building was demolished in 1843, to be replaced by the much larger and grander Italianate-style villa built by Charles Gray Round. This member of the Round family was a well-respected barrister and Member of Parliament for North Essex, as well as a great benefactor to the village. His legacy can be seen all over the parish. He provided the money to build the school and the new church as well as many domestic buildings that range from the rectory to the gatehouses to the park.

By the mid 20th century parts of the hall had become disused and were demolished leaving a single wing. In 2012 this building was altered and extended to create a suitable 21st century home on this historic site.

Back to my walk along Birch Brook, I took the path through the Birch Park woodland towards the church with its towering spire. As I approach this, the brook appears to divide into two and both small streams meander through an area of uneven ground. This is shown on the map as 'Pond Bay' in a script indicating it is a Non-Roman archaeological feature. The area has not been the subject of an archaeological investigation but the speculation is that the remains are mediaeval earthworks used as a dam for a mill or more likely to form fishponds or stews. A stew is a pond built specifically for the breeding, raising and storing of freshwater fish for eating. This site on Birch Brook is one of the most conspicuous features that remain of Birch Castle. Another feature is a short length of rampart and ditch on the higher ground just to the south of the church, in the grounds of a property called 'The Cottage'. Part of the area between these two ancient features is known the Bailey Meadow.

Although the castle is recorded to have been of the Norman motte and bailey type it is doubtful if the castle ever looked anything like the one depicted on the village sign. Morant states that Sir Ralph Gernon, 'fortified his castle of Briche against King Henry III'. This would have

The remains are mediaeval earthworks that were used as a dam for a mill or fishpond now retain only sufficient water for reeds and rushes to flourish. 2019

been sometime between 1216 and 1272. The majority of castles of the early Conquest period were of timber construction. Some were short-lived and others survived for centuries, with the timber buildings and defences being replaced sometimes in timber and sometimes in masonry. Again, there has been no archaeological investigation of the Birch site but it is thought the castle keep would only have been a timber structure with a wooden palisade, with another palisade surrounding the bailey.

Between the site of the dam and the castle stands the church of St Peter and St Paul. Although no longer used and falling into disrepair, we do not need to rely on speculation for its history. In 1849 the small mediaeval church, which stood on its elevated site, was in a dilapidated condition and was demolished. As previously mentioned, Charles Gray Round paid for the new church built on the same site. It is described by Pevsner as 'ambitious, but not showy'. An apt description that

A typical timber motte and bailey castle.

many will not appreciate until its towering spire disappears from the landscape, for this indeed is a possibility.

In 1960 the 110-foot (33m) spire was struck by lightning. This caused considerable damage and the top of the spire was replaced. It also revealed much decaying stonework, and other structural faults. In 1990 the church was formally closed after it was realized that there was no prospect of raising the £80,000 required to pay for the repairs to the crumbling tower. Four years later the Church Commissioners published a draft scheme for demolition. Since then there have been objections, several draft proposals to save the building and a proposed public enquiry. To date the future of the building remains uncertain.

The mediaeval church of St Peter & St Paul with its early lancet chancel windows, 14th century east window and slender, shingle spire. 1849

Mersea Museum/ Tony Millatt

*The interior of the closed church of
St Peter & St Paul, Birch. 2019*

*The church of St Peter & St Paul, Birch
awaiting re-use or demolition. 2019*

Birch Brook continues across the parish to the site of the former WWII airfield. The site at Birch was allocated in August 1942 to the US 8th Air Force for development into a heavy bomber base but construction work did not start until the following year when it became the last UK airfield to be built by the US. Its three concrete runways were built for heavy bombers and accommodation was provided for nearly 3,900 personnel. By the time that Birch Airfield was completed the need for airfields in East Anglia was satisfied and Birch became the airfield nobody wanted and it never got any aeroplanes. The RAF used it for a few days during early 1945 when 60 Dakota tugs and 60 Horsa gliders took off, but otherwise it saw little flying activity and closed soon after the end of the war.

Today most of the concreted areas have been removed, leaving single-track farm roads along some of the runways and parts of the

The bridge across Birch Brook at the site of the former Birch Bay Mill. 2019

perimeter track. Some hardstanding is used by Essex Council for garden waste composting and parts of the site are used as a solar farm.

There is little remaining of the wartime airfield that was never used so I made my way instead along Birch Street which ends at the parish boundary with Layer Breton and the *Hare & Hounds*.

After suitable sustenance I retraced my walk all the way back to Hill Farm. From there I took the track that leads down to Baymill. You need a keen eye to spot any evidence that such a building ever existed. There are a few bricks lurking in the undergrowth above the bridge that crosses Birch Brook. Across this bridge there is a bridleway leading off in the direction of Heckfordbridge. Before proceeding along there I will continue to explore the Baymill area.

The Chapman & Andre 1777 map shows two mills; one on Roman River and the other on Birch Brook, each a quarter-mile or so above

The bridge across Roman River at the site of the former Stanway Bay Mill. 2019

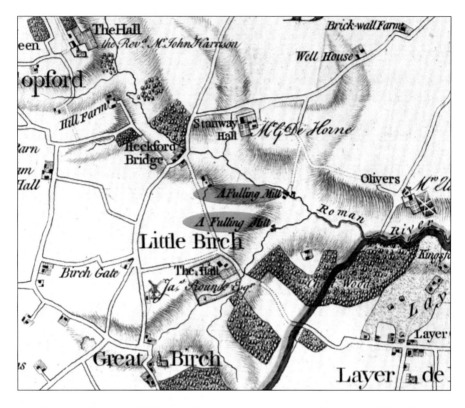

Chapman & Andre 1777 map showing two separate baymills; one on Birch Brook and the other on Roman River.

the confluence of the two rivers. Benham refers to the one on Roman River as the Stanway Mill and other as the Birch mill. The modern OS map conveniently prints 'Baymill' between the two sites. If the Birch Mill stood on the site of the mill mentioned in the Domesday book then this site has been used for milling since Saxon times. The Domesday records indicate that Stanway had three mills, so it seems likely that one of these was the Stanway Mill. During those early times the mills would have been used as corn mills and would not have changed to fulling until it was economical to do so.

There are records indicating the ownership of the Stanway Mill, variously known as the Fulling Mill, Bay Mill, Bays Mill or Cooper's Mill, from 1731 until 1803. This was a period during which the Essex cloth trade was in serious decline and many fulling mills changed to milling corn. Unfortunately this was not an option for the Roman River mills as the valley became depopulated. Both mills are shown on first edition OS map of 1805 but by the time of the 1893 revision both had disappeared.

Before I leave the parish of Birch, I will describe the crossing place less than a mile upstream from Stanway Mill called Heckfordbridge. This is where the B1022 main road between Colchester and Maldon crosses the Roman River. The small community that grew up around this crossing place has been called Heckford, Eckford, Hickford with the addition of Bridge as well as the single name, Heckfordbridge.

The first bridge across the river was for pedestrians only. Responsibility for its upkeep was shared between the owners of the land on either side of the river. An obligation they did not always fulfil. There are court records confirming this; the oldest dates back to 1631 when John Littlebury was accused of not repairing part of Heckford Bridge. This is followed by several more documents relating to the maintenance, more often the lack of it, until the wooden structure was replaced.

The first proposal for a carriage bridge was not made until 1824 when James Round of Birch Hall tried to persuade the County to pay for a bridge. He was not successful; it was another sixty-eight years before a brick-built carriage bridge replaced the timber footbridge. A contemporary description of the crossing place from around this time is illuminating, *'On reaching the foot of this hill, and ere he begins to ascend another, he must pass through a stream of water which runs merrily over a bed of shingle and gravel across the road…. the stream is crossed by one of those old and simple wooden bridges for the conveyance of foot passengers…. the bright and quiet-looking rivulet sometimes vindicates its claim to the rank of a river….for after a continuous rain, the waters hurry down and render the ford impassable either to man or horse.'*

Back at Baymill I am about to cross the river. Apart from my brief excursion to reach Layer Mill, I have not been north of the river since leaving Berechurch. Now I am about to cross the boundary of the pre-Roman settlement of Camulodunum that became Colchester. This covered parts of several parishes including the one I am about to enter.

An illustration of Heckford Bridge, viewed from the Birch Road, as it appears in the frontispiece of 'The Light of the Forge' by William Harrison. 1858

Heckford Bridge is now marked by tubular iron framework parapets. Beneath the widened carriageway are the remains of an earlier three arch brick structure. 2019

Mersea Museum/ Tony Millatt

A view of Heckford Bridge from the Maldon direction. pre1892

The existing reinforced concrete road bridge is built over a considerably narrower, earlier three arch brick bridge. The hard base of the ford is still discernible across the riverbed. 2019

CHAPTER 8

Stanway

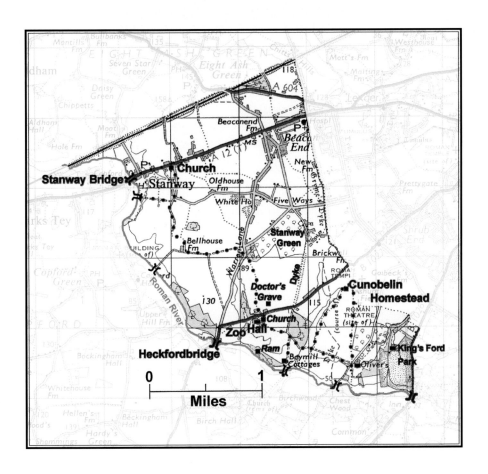

The church of St Albright is flanked by two former buildings, Oliver's barn and the toll-house together with an elephant and zebra representing the Zoo. The arms depicted beneath the village name include those of Colchester, the nearest we get to the recognition that the parish includes a considerable area of Camulodunum, the Iron Age settlement that became Britain's first city.

The name Stanway is derived from the ancient 'stone way' that became the Roman road that led from Colchester to London, which became the A12 until the bypass was built in 1971.

Recorded in the Domesday Book in 1086 as belonging to King Harold before the Conquest and William after. The manor always contained one mill.

In 1848 White described Stanway as a pleasant village on the north-eastern bank of the small Roman River, and on the London Road. It has many scattered houses, 807 inhabitants and 3368 acres of land.

The population of the parish of Stanway in 2011 was 8509.

Due to the importance of Roman River to the creation of Camulodunum and subsequently Colchester, Britain's first city, I considered giving Camulodunum a chapter of its own. However this would have broken the rather artificial constraint I have given myself of devoting each chapter to a particular Roman River Valley parish. The administrative centre of the Iron Age settlement lies within the modern parish of Stanway; which makes this the logical place for it appear.

I crossed Baymill Bridge into Stanway and followed the path up the steep side of the valley to the site of Bay Mill cottages. These rather isolated dwellings were inhabited until the 1960s since when they became dilapidated and were subsequently demolished and now all trace of their existence has been removed.

I stopped to look back over the valley, as the occupants of the cottages may have done, and many more before them, all the way back to pre-Roman times. The view would have been very different then; a landscape moulded by the Iron Age warriors to protect the territory of Cunobelin, the most powerful Iron Age ruler of southern Britain. I am within the outer defended area that enclosed his headquarters of Camulodunum. This inland promontory of some five square-miles of fertile plain is bounded by the River Colne, Roman River and a series of man-made dykes.

Here at the southwest corner of the territory is the site of the intersection of one of these dykes, Oliver's Dyke with Roman River. The steep-sided valley would have offered a similar protection to that of the dykes but it is likely to have been augmented by the encouragement of the growth of a dense thicket of gorse and thorny scrub. To encourage this growth and to provide a better view for the defenders, any shade creating trees growing on the steep sides of the valley would have been felled.

The managed thicket would have made the valley contours more apparent and the trees that now fill the valley would have been far more distant. I continue my walk along the bridleway following the line of the pre-Roman dyke that runs from the valley, past the site of the former cottages and way beyond towards the Colne. I followed in the footsteps of my Iron-Age ancestors, now across open farmland, then alongside the dyke, which has now been all but ploughed out of existence. On reaching Butcher's Wood a diminished profile of the dyke can be seen which is relatively well preserved as far as Stanway Green and beyond. I cross the stream into Oliver's Thicks and, following the valley, make my way towards Colchester's Archaeological Park. Before I reach this I notice, in the field on my right, the stubble of this year's harvest. As a chance coincidence, a long, dry summer and Google's surveying sequence has resulted in Google Earth's images of this area revealing crop marks. These show some of the droveways and buildings from the distant past. Within the northernmost area of the field is revealed a large rectangular enclosure. This is thought to have been Cunobelin's fortified homestead.

Before the Romans came to Britain there were no written records, so what little we know is from Roman accounts and interpretation of archaeological finds and features. New interpretations of our early history are constantly evolving but it is generally accepted that during the late 2nd century or early 1st century BC, a small band of Belgae fled northern Gaul and crossed to Britain and their culture quickly spread to most of lowland Britain. Their influence is confirmed by their style of pottery, use of coins and most importantly their oppida or enclosed spaces. These were large areas protected by massive dykes. The largest and best defended of them all was Camulodunum and this became the stronghold of Cunobelin.

Cunobelin controlled the industrial area closer to the River Colne where numerous artifacts were made and, it is estimated, over a million gold coins minted. Early peoples had a great veneration for water. This continued throughout the Iron Age and into the Roman period. It is not surprising that Cunobelin made his homestead within its fortified enclosure closer to Roman River and close by the sacred spring whose waters still flow down through Oliver's Thicks.

Close by Cunobelin's homestead, now over the hedge within the Archaeological Park, are the sites of a temple and theatre built after the arrival of the Romans. These may have replaced or augmented what was already a cultural and spiritual centre for the Trinovantes. Although nothing remains above ground of these buildings, their outlines have been marked in the grass and their imagined structure described on nearby information boards.

A gold coin struck at the Sheepen mint around 2,000 years ago. About the size of a modern 5p, it has an ear of wheat with the letters CAMU for Camulodunum and the reverse depicts a running horse with the letters CUNO for Cunobelin.

Chris Behn

Cunobelin was the undisputed leader of the Trinovantes whose territory covered Essex and a good part of Suffolk. As the leader of the most powerful tribe he was revered by the leaders of the other tribes of Britain to the extent that he has been referred to as the first King of the Britains. Cunobelin's memory was preserved in British legend and not recorded in writing until several centuries later. It was the information in these accounts that were the inspiration for Shakespeare's Cymbeline.

Passing through the Archaeological Park is Oliver's Lane, which leads to Oliver's Mansion. The present building has a grand Georgian façade but its origins date back to the 15th century. In the distant past, Oliver's was a manor in its own right and is named after Ralph Oliver, an early holder of the manor.

Oliver's Mansion 2013

Close by the mansion is Little Oliver's. This was formerly Oliver's Farm and retains the character of a plaster and weather-board clad 16th century, timber-framed building. This was for many years the home of the tenant farmers who worked the extensive estate.

It is not the first building to bear the name of Little Oliver's. This was first used for a rather grand early Victorian house that replaced a farmhouse way over to the east of Oliver's Lane. This house was accessed from the Layer road just above Kingsford Bridge, and the surrounding farmland was landscaped as a park. It was first known as Little Oliver's, then New Oliver's and by 1906 had become Kingsford Park. After ceasing to be a private residence it was, for many years, operated as the Kingsford Park Hotel before becoming Clarice House and is now the Bannatyne Health Club & Spa.

Little Oliver's, formerly Oliver's Farm. 2019

At the

Kingsford Park Hotel

Banqueting & Wedding Receptions.

Our experienced banqueting staff have been responsible for the smooth running and success of many wedding receptions, private parties, trade fairs, fashion shows, public meetings and dinner dances, and the Manager is always available, by appointment, to discuss the wide range of facilities.

Ristorante

We welcome you to a new experience in Mediterranean and Continental Cuisine, set in its own new Victorian conservatory style restaurant and commanding a picturesque view of the surrounding parkland

Layer Road (B1026) Colchester: 0206 34301

The Victorian building that was originally known as Little Oliver's had become Kingsford Park by 1906 which was later operated as an hotel as shown in this advertisement. 1991

Much of the land that is now the Archaeological Park was Oliver's Orchard. In 1983 some of the trees were removed and the land was ploughed for the first time for many years. The plough soon turned up a hoard of coins. The ploughman, Brian Wade, told the orchard owner, Rupert Knowles who immediately notified Colchester Museum who sent Assistant Curator, Mark Davies. Very soon museum staff and members of Colchester Archaeological Group had recovered not one but three separate hoards of over 6000 coins; thought to have been hidden towards the end of the 3rd century.

Oliver's Orchard has a special relevance to the much more recent story of the Roman River Valley. It was here that in 1982 the Roman River Centre opened and I became one of the many volunteers. The

The outward appearance of the Victorian building that now houses the Bannatyne Health Club & Spa has changed very little since it was built. 2019

centre housed information and interpretation exhibits of some of the many and varied aspects of the valley including its historic buildings, land use, history, geology, natural history. It was the information point for the conservation zone that had been established by Colchester Borough Council and Essex County Council in 1976. The zone consisted of an area of about eight square-miles between Rowhedge and Copford where the conservation, landscape management, archaeological and historic aspects would be coordinated by an advisory group representing all interested parties. Much has changed during the intervening years and the centre no longer exists but there have always been comings and goings in the valley, which is part of its charm.

I am now going to leave Oliver's Lane and make my way by bridleway to Stanway Hall, now the home of Colchester Zoo. Roman River Valley has a number of bridleways. Some of these are very ancient routes; some packhorse routes and others lead to farms or former farms. Today they are used by walkers, cyclists and horse riders but in the days of less mechanisation they were used by horsemen leading a laden beast or, having spent all day tilling the soil, they would lead the weary workhorse by its bridle back to the farm. Much of the land I walk over is now farmed by Stanway Hall Farm, which stands close by Stanway Hall. The farm and the hall remained in the same ownership until the end of WWII when the farm the hall with its grounds were sold separately.

Stanway Hall's elevated position overlooking the Roman River Valley can no longer be appreciated, surrounded as it is by the zoo's

Stanway Hall Farmhouse. 2019

numerous additional buildings and enclosures. The site may be that of the 13th century Stanway Castle whose location remains a mystery. It is certainly an ancient site on which stood the old hall when Sir John Swinnerton built his stately mansion on the site in 1610. Maybe it was too stately, as a subsequent owner considerably reduced its size. The present house dates from the late 1800s and is thought to have been built by Thomas Moy, Mayor of Colchester and wealthy coal merchant.

In 1963 F. M. Farrar acquired the hall and the surrounding land for a zoo. This later changed hands and by 1995 it housed over 150 species and attracted large numbers of visitors.

Adjacent to the hall, within the grounds of the zoo are the ruins of All Saints Church. The church tower has a relatively recent non-

Stanway Hall. 1960s

ecclesiastical connection to both the hall and Roman River. During the 19th century it housed a water tank that supplied the hall's drinking water. This was filled with drinking water supplied from a nearby spring by a hydraulic ram.

If you have been following my walk by using the OS Explorer map you may have noticed an area of woodland by Baymill Bridge called Ram Plantation, and within this appear the letters 'H Ram', which indicates the site of a hydraulic ram. It is no longer there but the ruins of the building that once housed it remain and fresh water still flows from the spring.

The hydraulic ram was developed in the late 1700s. The pump works by using the energy of a relatively large volume of water flowing through it to raise a small amount to a considerable height. They are made in a range of sizes from small units suitable for domestic

This building once housed the Ram that supplied drinking water to Stanway Hall. It was probably built during the late 19th century. 2019

installations, to large facilities to provide whole communities or large-scale irrigation systems. When the ram was installed at Stanway Hall it was to supply drinking water. This is why clean water from a small tributary stream fed from a spring, rather than Roman River's possibly polluted water, was used. The major advantage of the ram is that it does not require any additional power source for its operation. In remote locations far from an electricity supply or where it is difficult to supply coal or oil they are still used. And with increasing awareness of the environmental effects of the use of fossil fuels the demand for rams is increasing. Theoretically a ram can raise half of its water flow

The principle of operation is simple; it relies on the effect commonly known as water hammer. The heavy Ram valve (A) is normally held down and open by gravity. As the water flow increases the Ram is lifted and closes rapidly. This causes a sudden back-pressure, which opens the check valve (B). Water now flows into the pressure chamber and along the outlet pipe until the pressure drops and the check valve (B) closes. By now the Ram valve (A) has opened and the cycle is repeated.

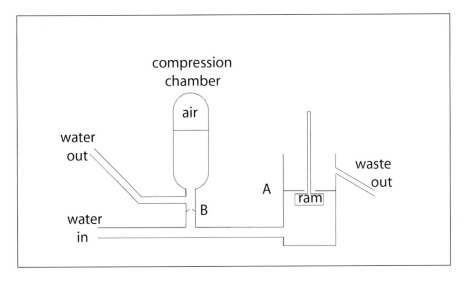

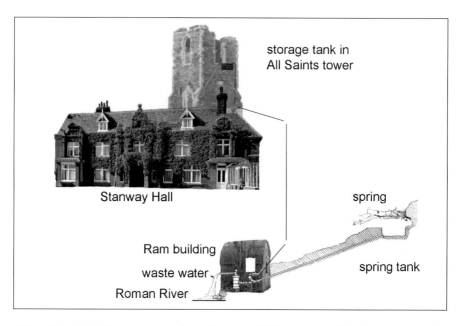

The original drinking water supply to Stanway Hall was supplied from a spring that emerged from the side of the Roman River valley nearly half-a-mile from the Hall. The spring water was collected in the spring tank, which had a pipe leading straight down the side of the valley to the Ram building. The Ram, powered by the flow enabled a proportion of the water to be pumped up to the storage tank housed in the tower of the redundant All Saints Church.

to twice the height it has fallen through, or a tenth to ten times the height. In practice they never quite achieve this because they operate at between 60% and 80% efficiency.

When the water storage tank was installed in the tower of All Saints the church had already been disused for many years. Nothing survives of the early 14th century church known to have been on this site; there are records of an early church being repaired in the 17th century but by the early 18th it was described as 'utterly decayed'.

Christina Edwards

All Saints, Stanway. 2001

Stanway has had its ups and downs. It was first recorded in 1002 and by 1066 it was held King Harold and was the centre of an estate that included parts of Lexden and Layer. By the Middle Ages, Stanway Hall and All Saint's Church were described as being in Great Stanway. Little Stanway was served by a chapel dedicated to St Ethelbert, King of the East Angles, which later became known as St Albright's. By 1790 the rector reported that there was no village or hamlet in the whole of Stanway. And so it remained, a sparsely populated scattered settlement, until the 19th century. Then the expansion Colchester produced ribbon development and infilling which accelerated during the 20th century and continues to this day.

Across the road from the zoo I take the track that soon becomes a footpath as it crosses extensive gravel workings. We call these sand and gravel pits, which sounds better than opencast mining but that is what it is. Before this activity started the fields concealed hidden treasure of a different sort. These were discovered by aerial photography in 1932 but not excavated until 1992-6 when archaeological investigation took place, prior to the expansion of the sand and gravel extraction activity. It was soon revealed that the site was a remarkable burial site dating from the time when the importance of Camulodunum was at its height, until some time after the arrival of the Romans. No one was expecting the site to include such remarkable burials as were uncovered. One of the earliest and most significant burials was that of a doctor whose

The Tarmac Quarry at Stanway produces sands and gravels for a wide range of building products. Material from here has been used in many local developments including the extension of Abberton Reservoir, the building of Colchester United Football Stadium and the rebuilding of Colchester Garrison. Material is transported further afield by rail from the company's sidings at Marks Tey.

grave goods included a surgical kit and a board game. The instruments were the first of their type to have been discovered and indicated that the individual was a Briton and was soon described as the 'Druid of Colchester' in the popular press. Indeed the instruments revealed how sophisticated the surgical abilities and practices of the Celts were before the arrival of the Romans. The board game, which gained much of the international media attention, was set out with pieces as if in play. It has been suggested that the absence of dice indicates this was a game of strategy rather than chance. This was obviously thought to be significant to the individual for it to be included with his grave goods.

The ancient right of way with concealed deep water on either side as it approaches Furze Hill. Tarmac's current plan is to restore the area, over a twenty-year period, to 'a wildlife-enhanced agricultural and water-based landscape, with improved public access and woodland planting for the people of Colchester and the surrounding communities to enjoy.'

My path continues past the site of these finds and soon crosses the access road to the most recent working area. The narrow strip of the ancient route, still marked by an earth bank and a few boundary oaks, passes high above its new surroundings. On either side are the exhausted earlier workings. In some of these nature is reasserting itself, sometimes with a little help from its despoilers.

At Furze Hill I cross Warren Lane to continue along the footpath across what appears to be open heathland towards Bellhouse Farm. This is indeed impoverished land, a thin covering of soil over tons of decaying 20th century rubbish used to fill even earlier gravel pits.

I am back on relatively undisturbed land by the time I reach Bellhouse Farm. This is a surprisingly large collection of farm buildings

The footpath from Furze Hill towards Bellhouse Farm crosses acres of infilled former gravel workings. 2019

The infilling continues in the distance; in the foreground is part of the collection unit for the methane produced from the buried decaying organic matter. Landfills usually produce appreciable amounts of gas within three years rising to a peak after a further three or four after which gas continues to be emitted for up to 50 years. 2019

of various ages, now used by a variety of enterprises. Set in rural tranquility away from public roads the present farmhouse dates from the late 16ᵗʰ century. This replaced a much earlier dwelling, the name itself is a corruption of Belhus from Thomas deBelhus who held the Manor of Stanway in 1274.

Evidence of occupancy even further back in time was indicated by an extensive area of crop marks. These, in fields just to the southwest of the farmhouse towards Roman River, were investigated by the Colchester Archaeological Group in 1999. This revealed a ditched circular enclosure and post-holes indicating the presence of a large round-house some ten metres in diameter dating from the late Neolithic and early Bronze Age. Other finds indicate that the site was continuously occupied from the late Iron Age to the end of the Romano-British period in the mid 3rd century.

From the farmhouse I walk along the surfaced concrete track towards Church Lane. Just before the path joins Church Lane at Digomy Corner, a track to the left leads to the site of one of the former Stanway mill, North's Mill. Although in Stanway this mill belonged to Copford so I will leave my description of the site for the following chapter. Meanwhile I retrace my steps back to Church Lane and along to the church located in an area that at was once referred to as Little Stanway.

St Albright's is the only church in the country to be dedicated to this little known Saxon saint. The name is a corruption of St Ethelbert and it is not certain if this is St Ethelbert, King of Kent (d.597) or St Ethelbert, King of the East Angles (d.793). The building whose origins date from the 12th century had many later additions including the attractive 17th century bell turret before being heavily restored by the Victorians. The lych gate was built as a war memorial in 1920.

From the church it is downhill along London Road to where it crosses Roman River by Stanway Bridge. This used to be called Elpeford or Emperford until 1580 when it acquired its present name. It was a footbridge that was probably rebuilt several times until 1808 when the first carriage bridge was built, which is a long time after the road was turnpiked in 1696.

Much of the original bridge survives to this day and many people cross it unaware of its existence. The road is flat and barely narrows as it crosses Roman River between the *Swan Inn* in Stanway and the ruins of Copford Place in Copford. As far as I know the river has always been the boundary between these two parishes at this point.

St Albright's, Stanway. 2019

The road is now the B1408. Until the Copford and Stanway bypass was opened in the 1971 it was the A12 and before that the ancient Roman road, Stane Street, that connected Colchester to St Albans. The bridge is a single arch brick structure surmounted by plain brick parapets with capstones. On one of these is inscribed a benchmark. Nowadays, a benchmark has come to mean any reference point or standard to which to refer or aspire. This meaning is derived from the accuracy with which the original bench marks were installed by the Ordnance Survey. The one on Stanway Bridge is shown on early maps as B.M.83.4. This indicates it is exactly 83.4 feet (25.42m) above sea level.

The ancient Stane Street that became the A12 and since 1971 the B1408 as it crosses the bridge over Roman River between Stanway and Copford. 2018

This led me to wonder what was the sea level referred to. Was it the level of the sea in the tidal reaches of Roman River at Fingringhoe Mill? Would it be measured when the tide is in, or out, or somewhere in between? What about the effect of all the freshwater flowing into the river? And what about global rising sea level? So what does B.M.83.4 actually mean? The first known sea level measurements were made nearly 400 years ago by Jeremiah Horrocks at Toxteth. A century later, William Hutchinson recorded the height of every tide for thirty years at Liverpool Old Dock. When the Ordnance Survey was established in 1791 a national system of height measurement was needed and the first levelling survey was started, based on the average sea level at Liverpool. This was measured using a gauge, a mechanical float in a stilling well, installed in a tide house at the Victoria Dock.

The Stanway-Copford bridge from the riverbank. 2018

As measuring became more accurate and mapping standards improved, changes in land levels and sea levels became more important. Consequently a new levelling survey was started in 1912. This was to be based on a new sea level determined from data collected at three new Tidal Observatories at Dunbar, Newlyn and Felixstowe. The data collected during the ensuing few years showed unpredictable variation in the sea level of the North Sea. This led to the decision that Newlyn would be used as the national sea level datum level. An unassuming shed close to the lighthouse on the south pier of the harbour is Britain's tidal observatory. It houses the tide gauge and a simple brass bolt set in rock-solid Cornish granite in a recess in the floor. The top of this domed bolt is the bench mark for all height measurements in mainland Britain. The bench mark on Stanway Bridge is one of the network of 750,000 bench marks positioned by the Ordnance Survey.

Over the bridge is my next parish, the parish of Copford.

The Ordnance Survey bench mark on the southwest corner of the parapet of Stanway-Copford Bridge. 2018

CHAPTER 9

Copford

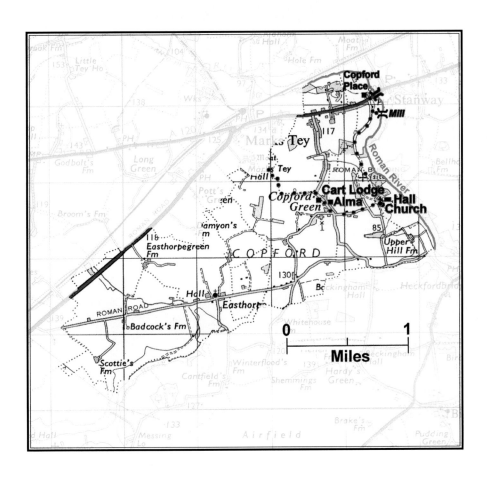

This sign features the church and the cart lodge with an oak tree, probably the ancient specimen on the cricket field. The shield of the City of London represents the ancient links of the manor with the Bishops of London.

The name Copford is thought to be derived from the name of a Saxon, Coppa who controlled an area around where Roman River was crossed, hence Coppa's ford that became Copford.

Recorded in the Domesday Book in 1086 as Coppeforda, it was held by the Bishop of London.

In 1848 William White described Copford as a pleasant parish of scattered houses containing 645 inhabitants and 2350 acres.

The population of the parish of Copford in 2011 was 1689.

Before I leave the river, I will just mention that in Saxon times the land around here was probably controlled by a Saxon named Coppa and the crossing over the river would have been Coppa's ford, which over the years has become shortened to Copford.

The first house on the Copford side of the river is Copford Place. This is a timber-framed 18ᵗʰ century house with a gault brick façade with later extensions. In 1947 it was converted into private accommodation for the elderly. In 1980 it was taken over by Help the Aged and refurbished in 1998; then a few years later it ceased to be in use. Since when the site has been the subject of various plans for development during which time the building has become increasing derelict. This is a Grade 2 listed building, which means that it cannot be demolished or altered in any way without Listed Building consent. However, there is no legal requirement on the owner to carry out repairs or maintenance. And as far as this building is concerned there appears to have been little in the way of either and it is now approaching a condition beyond repair. This seems to be a strange way to protect our heritage.

It is becoming increasingly likely that this listed building will suffer the same demise as many others and through decay release a valuable site for new development. It would be nice if we could be sure that this will enhance this desirable riverside location.

A little further along the road is the site of Copford windmill. This was the subject of a painting by John Constable, which for many years was described as Stanway Mill because this is where the artist said it was. This may have been because he did not realize that Roman River divides the two parishes. It is likely that he could have broken one of his many stagecoach journeys from London to East Bergholt at one of the Stanway hostelries.

Traditionally the parish maintained roads within a parish. This system, although often subject to dispute, worked relatively well until

Copford Place as a residential hotel in 1955

Copford Place. 2011

Copford Place. 2018

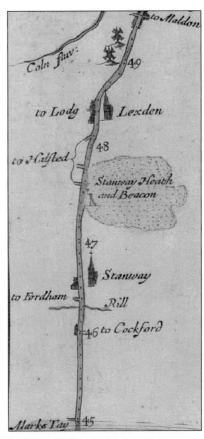

The Copford - Stanway section of the 1675 linear map of the London to Harwich Road by John Ogilby.

Christina Edwards

long distance travel increased and the variation in the standards of maintenance between parishes became apparent. The solution was to establish Turnpike Trusts with powers to collect a toll from those who used the road, to pay for its maintenance. When John Constable travelled this road it had been turnpiked since the late 1600s. This was one of the earliest Trusts in the land; it was set up to maintain the road between London and Harwich. At the time England was at war with France but had close links, both royal and commercial, with the Low Countries. One of the obligations of a Turnpike Trust was to mark their route with milestones. This fact was noted by Count Frederick Kielmansegge who in 1761 wrote in his diary *'it was 72*

The Tollgate Cottage that stood at Stanway until the 1970s. The door, originally on the roadside was flanked by splayed windows, which gave a good view along the road in both directions.

English miles from Harwich to London each of which is marked by a large stone, on which the figures of the distances from London are cut.'

One of these stones, number 46, was in Copford with numbers 47 and 48 in Stanway. Stanway also had a tollgate where the dues from travellers were collected. This was often a long bar that could be raised, similar those used at some car parks, but back then likened to the long pole or pike used by infantry.

The Copford milestone is long gone as are the two in Stanway. More disappointing is the loss of the Stanway tollgate cottage, which was unnecessarily demolished in 1970s during the construction of the Tollgate roundabout and the development of the Tollgate retail park.

Almost opposite Copford Place is Hall Road that follows the river downstream. A short distance along here is a footpath that leads

Christina Edwards

Watermill Cottages from the Copford side of the river, which flows unseen between the photographer and the cottages. ~1930

down to the site of the former Stanway Mill, sometimes referred to as North's, Smith's or Machin's Mill. The mill appears to have belonged to the Manor of Copford, although it stood within the parish of Stanway. In 1692 it was described as watermill, dwelling and three acres of meadow. A mere sixteen years later the mill was described as *a waste*. It appears to have been repaired or rebuilt as it featured in a will of 1735. Subsequent records are not clear, leaving the date of its demise and precise location unclear. A pair of timber-framed cottages known as Watermill Cottages, which were very likely to have been on the site of an earlier building were being used as farm workers cottages until the 1930s. The millponds have long gone but the lie of the land gives some clue as to their possible locations.

The foot bridge over Roman River near the site of Watermill Cottages which would have stood in the trees in the left background. 2019

Back to Hall Road and the Anglia Water treatment plant. This facility, which deals with the treatment of sewage and water from the ever-expanding population of the parish, is now working at full capacity and the site cannot be enlarged without having a detrimental impact on the small river and valley in which it is situated.

Shortly past the treatment plant the surfaced road comes to an end but the ancient thoroughfare, now designated as a footpath, continues as an unmade track. It is thought that this route dates from Roman, or possibly even earlier times as a link road between Stane Street and the other parallel southern route to Colchester through Easthorpe, and along Maldon Road past the zoo.

At about the mid-point of this link road was some sort of Roman settlement near the present parish church of St Michael & All Angels.

The Church of St Michael & All Angels, Copford. 2019

A substantial part of this impressive building dates from the early 12th century and contains a large amount of re-used Roman bricks, tiles and hypocaust fragments from the earlier buildings. It is likely that this was not the first church to have been built here, as it is known the manor of Copford was held by the Bishops of London under the Saxon Kings and remained in their ownership after the Norman Conquest.

The most likely explanation for the rebuilding of the church and extremely high quality of its workmanship and artistry worthy of any cathedral or abbey, is that early Norman bishops regularly resided in the manor and the church was built as their chapel. Many of the original wall paintings have been restored and are undoubtedly the most impressive to be seen in any parish church in the country.

One of the many exceptional wall paintings in Copford Church,
'Christ in Majesty'. 2019

As I entered the church by the south door, I was reminded of stories I had forgotten about the church door being covered with human skin. I was relieved to learn upon reading the church guide that these stories did not relate to the door through which I had entered.

The original, ancient south door was removed in the early 20th century and is now hung in one of the north entrances and best viewed from outside. From here it can be seen that its elaborate metal hinges have been restored in places. It was traditional practice to place cattle hide between the wood of the door and the iron of the hinge to protect the wood. During an earlier restoration during the 1700s pieces of thin parchment were found under the hinges. This discovery was seen to confirm the local story that a marauding Dane was caught plundering the church, was flayed and his skin attached to the door as a deterrent to others. Historians pointed out that the church door, as old it maybe, is unlikely to date back the times of marauding Danes. If, indeed it was human skin, it is more likely to be that of a poacher whose punishment at the time the door was made would have been flaying.

Copford is not the only church door to be associated with a gruesome human skin legend. There does seem to be some sort of folk memory

Copford Church door is reputed to have been covered with human skin. 2019

associated with marauding Danes that is manifested in different, but similar, stories in several locations.

Forensic examination performed in the late 20th century proves that the parchment fragments from the Copford door belonged to a fair-skinned male. DNA analysis of other samples from other churches have revealed that some are human and others not. As yet, none have been dated but as far as Copford is concerned there is the possibility that the hinges were removed with skin attached from an earlier door and reapplied to the new Norman door. Whatever the truth, the clear message in all the stories is, don't steal from churches.

The hall, a stately red-brick Georgian house in attractive grounds, is built adjacent to the church, on the site of an earlier building that was used as a residence of the Bishops of London.

Copford Hall undergoing restoration viewed from the church. 2019

The front of the hall overlooks an extensive green, adjacent to which is the village cricket pitch. Rather unusually, if not uniquely, within its boundary stands one of the majestic oaks for which the parish is renowned.

From the cricket pitch I walked the short distance along Church Lane to Copford Green with its younger oak. This was planted to commemorate the coronation of Edward VII in 1902. A few years later it was joined by one of the County's earliest cast-iron signposts. Today this is one of no more than a dozen that survive. The name Stanton can just about be made out under the peeling paint of the shaft. Another characteristic of the signposts cast by this Derbyshire foundry are the rounded ends of the arms, which include a space for a road number.

Copford Cricket Pitch. The umpire keeping an eye on the game from under the famous oak. 2019

The road numbering system was based on the idea of an ever-branching tree with a few trunk roads, several of which emanated from London. Each of these had side branches and those that were up to a certain standard were classified as A roads. Smaller roads branching off the A roads were B roads and those branching off these were sometimes designated with C, D or U, which stood for unclassified. Very few of these later designations ever appeared on signposts. This system of road numbering was not introduced until the formation of the Ministry of Transport in 1919.

The signpost on Copford Green, with its circular roundel bearing the Essex County Council name, dates from 1919. Shortly after this, the lucrative contract for supplying cast-iron direction posts in Essex was awarded to the Maldon Ironworks.

The cast-iron signpost on Copford Green was one of the earliest to be erected by Essex County Council. 2019

The Alma. *2019*

Although now relatively rare, many more of the designs from this foundry survive. Most are easily recognized by their semi-circular top, which often bears the parish name.

Overlooking the green is the popular village pub, which has been both The Lion and The George and is now *The Alma*, named after the Crimean battle that took place in 1854. Here I took a welcome break before visiting the last of my list of Copford attractions. This is the cart lodge, once a common feature in most villages. There are now few survivors and the one in Copford, within sight of the Alma, is one of the best. Its 17th century frame has traditional weather-boarded gables and a thatched roof that encloses a hayloft. It stands alongside the pond whose sloping sides would have allowed easy access to the wooden wheeled carts. Traditionally a wooden wheel consisted of an

The 17th century Copford cart lodge with the pond and Alma beyond. 2019

elm hub, ash spokes and an oak rim made up from segments, each of which was called a felloe. These were all held together with an iron tyre. To keep the wheel tight in dry weather, carts were allowed to stand in water to allow their felloes to swell. A scene immortalised in Constable's Haywain.

A short distance along the road there is a footpath, the only footpath that connects Copford to its neighbouring parish of Marks Tey.

The footpath from Copford, across fields towards Marks Tey. 2019

CHAPTER 10

Marks Tey

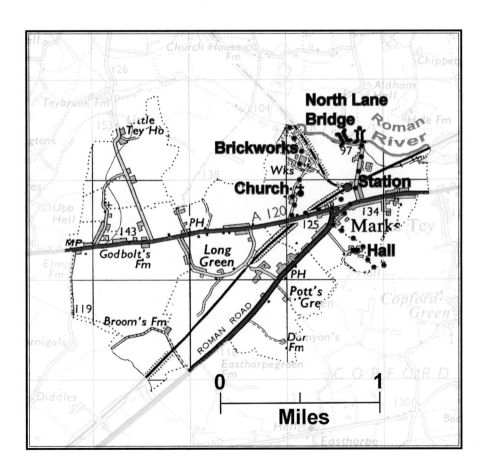

St Andrew's Church, the railway, aspects of brickmaking and horticulture along with the arms of the Borough of Colchester and the County of Essex.

Tey is thought to be derived from the Old English word 'tiege' or 'teag' meaning an enclosure. After the Conquest the area called Tey was given to Geoffrey de Mandeville and part of this land was held under him by the de Merk family who became lords of the manor. The area then became known as Marks Tey.

Recorded in the Domesday Book in 1086 as Tey, it was held by Geoffrey de Manderville.

In 1848 White described Marks Tey, or Tey at the Elms as a pleasant village on the London Road and served by the Eastern Counties Railway. It has 397 inhabitants and 1214 acres of rich soil.

The population of the parish of Marks Tey in 2011 was 2551.

As I walked across the fields along the footpath that connects the two parishes of Copford and Marks Tey, I wondered for how much longer such rural scenes will remain a feature of the area. The Roman River valley has long provided a breathing space for the surrounding communities. However an ever-expanding Colchester has urbanized much of Stanway and is now creeping along the London Road into Copford.

It would be nice to think that the proposed development of a 'garden village' at West Tey will respect the benefit to urban communities of green space. However, developers seldom actually live in their own developments and the quality of life of future residents appears to have a low priority, compared to the extra profit that can be made by squeezing in an extra few buildings. The idea of a garden village sounds attractive, but the reality of 15,000 new homes with an expected population of about 40,000 people is in fact a conurbation over twice the size of Witham.

It all started a long time ago. The very name Tey is thought to be derived from a Saxon word 'tiege' or 'teag', meaning an enclosure that was probably a cleared area within a forest. In Saxon times forest covered most of Essex. After the Conquest in 1066 land was given to the noblemen who had helped William the Conqueror. Tey was given to Geoffrey de Mandeville and part of this land was held under him by the de Merk family, who became lords of the manor. Historically, the area has been referred to as Tey Mandeville, or Tey at Elms from the many elm trees that flourished on the heavy clay soil. Eventually, it became known as Marks Tey.

I was now approaching Marks Tey Hall, which was for many years the seat of the lords of the manor. This is an ancient moated site and there has been a house here since at least 1307. Part of the moat survives and parts of the existing house date from the 16th century, as

A view into Marks Tey from the parish boundary that runs across the foreground.
The path crosses a hay field adjacent to Marks Tey Hall. 2019

does the nearby South Barn. The hall ceased to be a manorial seat a long time ago. It was for many years used as a farmhouse but is now derelict and falling into disrepair.

It looks as if, at one time, there could have been a direct route between the hall and the church. Today the footpath leaves the hall in the direction of the parish Church of St Andrew, but now, after a short distance, ends at the slip-road on to the A12. Marks Tey has always been a place to go through, and many of these through routes run between the hall and the church. Traffic would have increased with the turnpiking of the Harwich to London road followed a few years later by the Stane Street turnpike to Braintree. The increased traffic allowed the local inns to flourish. Then in 1841 the railway arrived, and the route chosen divided the village. The later line to Sudbury caused further division. And most recently, the dueling of the A12 has further segmented the community.

The 16th century Marks Tey Hall, a Grade II listed building falling into disrepair. 2019

The Grade II listed Marks Tey Hall South Barn that was built ~1525 is now in need of some care and maintenance. 2019

The footpath as it leaves The Hall in the direction of St Andrew's Church. Between this field of buttercups and the church is the A12, the railway and the A120. 2019

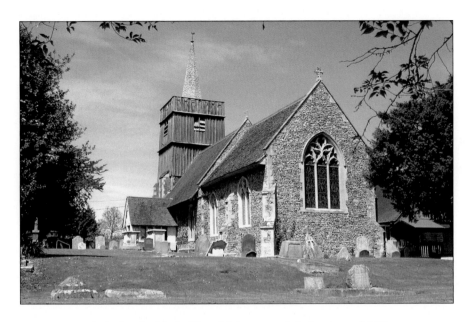

St Andrew's, Marks Tey with its unusual timber tower. 2019

From the A12 slip-road, I can only reach the church by following busy roads. Fortunately there are pavements most of the way. But the route is tortuous along the B1408, over the footbridge across the A12 duel-carriageway then along the A120 and over the railway bridge. Eventually I reach the quieter Church Lane that leads to St Andrew's Church.

The church is built on an ancient site that could well have been revered in pre-Christian times. It now stands somewhat isolated, in relative tranquillity. In former times it could well have been at the centre of the community. Parts of the building date from the 12th century and include much re-used Roman brick. Its most notable feature is its 15th century tower; this stone and brick structure was virtually demolished during the siege of Colchester in 1648 after which the upper stages were rebuilt in timber. The enormous corner posts are clad with elm boards. The tower is surmounted by a spire whose oak shingles had to be replaced as result of WWII bomb-blast damage.

I continued along Church Lane to the brickworks. During my travels along the valley I have mentioned various sites where bricks have been made in the past. These span every period during which bricks have been manufactured, from Roman times to the Victorian period. Due to the paucity of natural stone in the area, brick is an important building material. Once made, it is as enduring as many types of building stone. There are a number of sites within the valley where there is clay suitable for brickmaking. The only one currently

The clay used for brickmaking at the W H Collier site. This glacial, alluvial deposit formed in lake basin during the most recent ice age. Deposits were laid down over a 20,000 year period from meltwaters, during the interglacial period about a million years ago. 2019

in use is here in Marks Tey where W H Collier Ltd have been digging clay from their site since 1863.

The Romans brought the art of brickmaking to Britain. When they left, the art was lost until the arrival of the Flemings towards end of the 15th century. Since then the basic process has remained substantially unchanged.

Clay is dug in the autumn and allowed to over-winter in heaps, being turned over several times to allow it to weather. Sand and water is then mixed with the clay. In the early days this was done by treading. Later a pug mill was used; a horse usually drove these early mills; modern pug mills are driven by electricity. The brick maker then kneads the mixture prior to throwing it into a sanded mould with sufficient force to fill the mould. The surplus clay is removed and the newly formed brick extracted from the mould. The bricks are then dried. This used to be done in the open, and then later in open-sided sheds called hacks where drying took up to 6 weeks. W H Collier bricks are now dried in ten days on trucks, which move slowly through chambers built above a tunnel kiln. This is no longer operational and the

The original downdraught kiln built in 1883 on the Collier site. It was used to fire bricks, flowerpots, land drain pipes and roofing tiles. 2019

heat is now provided by LPG gas burners instead of the waste heat from the tunnel kiln. The dried bricks are then fired. In the early days this was done in a clamp, which was a skillfully built pile of layers of brushwood and unfired bricks all enclosed in a layer of fired bricks. The completed clamp was set alight on the windward side and left to burn uncontrollably for several weeks. This often resulted in large numbers of spoilt bricks. Later, kilns were introduced; these were still fired with wood. For many years W H Collier used a tunnel kiln through which the trucks of bricks passed in 3½ days during which time they were heated to over 1000 degrees before going through a period of controlled cooling. The firing is now performed in a moving hood kiln, which takes a similar length of time but is more convenient for small batch production. This is the final stage in transforming soft malleable clay into a hard and extremely durable material, capable of lasting for hundreds of years.

The brickworks is at the end of Church Lane. To continue my exploration of the parish I need to retrace my steps back past the church and along the A120 to the railway station. This is now a smart glass affair, very different to the original station building, which was built by the Eastern Counties Railway (ECR) in 1841. This was the first railway to be built in the region and was intended to go between London and Norwich but as the line approached Colchester two things happened. Firstly the ECR ran into financial difficulties causing the line to terminate at Colchester. Secondly, the embankment at Stanway was not up to standard and this resulted in the dismissal of the engineer responsible, who was the thirty-year-old Peter Bruff. This dismissal gave the ambitious young engineer the opportunity to build the railway past Colchester to Ipswich. To do this he secured funding from a consortium of Ipswich businessmen and thus the Eastern Union Railway (EUR) was born, with Peter Bruff as resident engineer.

Dried bricks about to enter Collier's tunnel kiln for firing. 2002

Unfired bricks stacked on the hearth of the moving hood kiln.
The hood (behind) moves on rails to encase them while they are fired. 2019

Shenfield to Ipswich by Vic Mitchell (www.middletonpress.co.uk)

Marks Tey Station. c1910

Marks Tey Station. 2019

Shenfield to Ipswich by Vic Mitchell (www.middletonpress.co.uk)

Marks Tey Station with the main line on the left and the Stour Valley line to the right. 1950s

The semaphore signals have been replaced and all the gantries associated with main line electrification have been erected. 2019

Peter Bruff was a man of his time who was passionate about the advantages that civil engineering projects could bring to communities. He also had the personality to successfully persuade local dignitaries and businessmen to back his schemes. In practically every town in the region his name crops up in connection with one project or another. In Harwich he was responsible for the town's harbour works, the town's first pier, and the water works. Shortly after completing these projects he bought a house and a considerable amount of land in the coastal town of Walton-on-the-Naze. Here he set about putting down an artesian well and installing steam engines to pump water to the whole of the town. He built sea defences with concrete walks. He built houses and an hotel as well as a gasworks to provide street lighting.

Then he bought a large stretch of deserted coastline near to the inland village of Clacton. Here he planned to build a completely new town, Clacton-on-Sea. His grand plan was for the town to be an ideal seaside resort. Unrestrained by existing roads or buildings he designed the road layout and then started separate companies to build an hotel and a public hall. When he sold off individual building plots he laid down strict covenants and kept control of all services. He was, in effect, a one-man planning committee who kept control of all the town facilities, including drainage and paving, open spaces and the design of the buildings that overlooked them. The whole of the town centre, even today, is Bruff's town centre. The town began as a decorous Victorian resort in accordance with his wishes, with villas occupied by genteel families, and hotels and boarding houses visited by similar folk. But the introduction of 'bank holidays', in 1871, brought a conflicting element, day-trippers who arrived in droves, first by steamer and then by train. I often wonder what Bruff thought about the inevitable change to his genteel creation brought about by the easy access he had inadvertently provided with his own creations of piers and railways.

Some years later his interest in Clacton-on-Sea waned and he restricted his activities to the design and construction of sewerage and water systems. These included a sewer system for Ipswich, the town in which he had lived since his early days with the EUR, and an improved water system for Colchester that included the landmark water tower 'Jumbo'. When Peter Bruff died in 1900, he had managed to leave his mark in just about every town in eastern England and had built Clacton-on-Sea from nothing, but his most monumental work is his viaduct at Chappel.

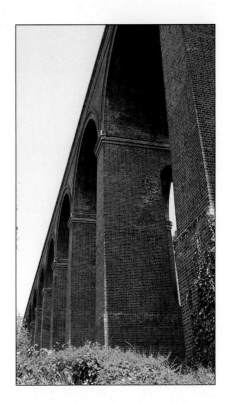

The major obstacle on the proposed railway line between Marks Tey and Sudbury was the Colne Valley. Peter Bruff decided that this could be crossed by a viaduct and set about preparing a suitable design. This was to consist of a series of laminated wooden arches supported on brick piers. Then the discovery of a nearby plentiful supply of brickearth persuaded him to abandon these plans in favour of an all brick one. Work started in July 1847 and a mere twenty months later some seven million bricks had been laid to create, what was at the time the largest brick structure in the country.

The 32 arch Chappel Viaduct contains some seven million bricks and towers 75ft(23m) above the village. 2014

Peter Bruff (1812-1900), the Brunel of the Eastern Counties.

Roman River as it enters the large culvert under the Marks Tey to Sudbury railway in the grounds of W H Collier's brickworks.

Crossing the Roman River Valley did not present the same sort of challenge. In the grounds of W H Collier's brickworks the river flows under the railway through no more than a large culvert.

The road continues past the station as North Lane to Roman River, which is the parish boundary. The river is crossed in two places. I will first visit the new road bridge. This was built in 2019 to replace an earlier less sturdy structure with its adjacent ford.

The new bridge incorporates an otter ledge, which I hope the otters will use. These animals were almost driven to extinction by human activity, pesticides and pollution. Thankfully, the measures taken since the 1970s have enabled them to make an extraordinary comeback. This has happened as a result of legislation making it an offence to kill otters and banning the use of certain pesticides which has resulted in an improvement in the quality of the water in the nation's waterways.

These factors, together with subtle habitat improvements, have allowed otters to return to many of our rivers including Roman River. One of the main dangers they now face is one I have inadvertently shared with them during my walk through Marks Tey; that of crossing the road. For some reason these animals do not like swimming under bridges, preferring instead to run across the road. So, hopefully, the provision of the otter ledge will keep death off this piece of new road.

To use the second river crossing to proceed into the next parish, I will walk back along the road to the fingerpost that indicates the footpath leading to Aldham Hall. The path passes through a small, uncultivated wilderness before crossing the river by a concrete footbridge into the parish of Aldham.

The iron girder North Lane Bridge shortly before demolition in 2018.

The new reinforced concrete North Lane Bridge protected by rock-filled gabions. Those that extend under the bridge form an otter ledge. This provides a safe route for otters to cross the road. 2019

The footbridge has a neat concrete step and metal bar forming a stile at each end. Across Roman River the path continues to Aldham Hall hidden in the distance. 2018

CHAPTER 11

Aldham

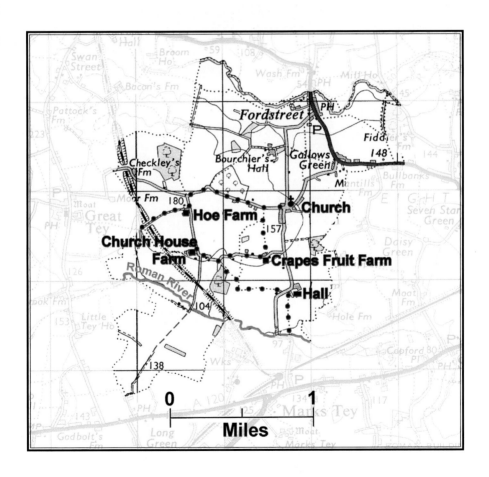

This iron village sign depicts the church of St Margaret & St Catherine. Above the head of its most famous Rector, the Essex historian, Philip Morant, behind him the apple tree represents the significance of parish orchards. The parish name sits upon the profile of a bridge that represents the Fordstreet area of the parish.

The name Aldham combines two Saxon words, which means old village. It has been variously recorded as Aldenham, Audeham and Audham.

Recorded in the Domesday Book in 1086 as Aldeham from the Saxon Old-ham or old village. After the Conquest it was held by Odo, Bishop of Bayeux, brother of the Conqueror. By 1086 it was in the hands of the ancestors of the Earls of Oxford.

In 1848 William White described Aldham as a small pleasant village of 382 souls and 1790 acres of fertile land.

The population of the parish of Aldham in 2011 was 491.

The footpath crosses a small meadow and then follows a field edge up to Aldham Hall. This is the oldest house in the parish and could well have been built on the site of the earlier mediaeval settlement of 'old ham' from which the parish takes its name. The present house is a substantial early 15th century timber-framed and plastered structure under a red peg-tiled roof. Over the years it has had many additions and alterations but remains an attractive building. The pond to its west may well be the remains of a moat.

Somewhat unusually, the Hall is situated some way from the site of the original parish church. But the two sites are connected by what remains a reasonably direct public footpath. This pleasant walk, across open countryside, affords good views of the upper Roman River Valley before passing Church House Wood to the nearby Church House Farm. On old maps this is marked as the centre of Aldham and its

Aldham Hall retains many of its original Elizabethan features. 2019

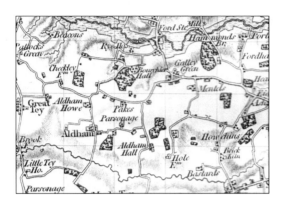

On this OS map of 1805 Aldham is shown as being at the site of Church House Farm.

Roy Fulcher Collection

The old church of St Margaret & St Catherine, Aldham which was demolished in 1854.

Today there is no indication that a church with numerous grave stones once occupied this site. 2019

church overlooked the Roman River Valley. At one time a cluster of dwellings surrounded the church but most of these had disappeared by the time the old church was demolished in 1894, leaving only Church House Farm to survive into the 20th century.

The original Aldham church, parts of which were built in the early 13th century, was never smart and often in a state of disrepair. Due to this and the fact that over the years the scattered population of the parish had migrated away from the old site, it was decided to build a new church closer to the new centres of population. The new church was opened in 1855 and was built to much the same plan as the old one with many of the original materials re-used. These included 13th and 14th century windows and the beautifully carved 14th century porch, which was moved in its entirety.

I have a choice of routes to reach the new church and will choose the lane that takes me past Crapes Fruit Farm. This was established in 1922 and continues to be run by the founder's grandson, Andrew Tann. The farm is dedicated to the production of quality apples and other fruit of many traditional English varieties. Andrew, the eldest of the third generation of Tanns at the farm, is dedicated to the production of apples - which taste like apples should. The fruit farm has a collection of over 150 varieties of apple, which was compiled by Andrew's father, John Tann. These include both traditional and lesser-known varieties such as Blenheim Orange, D'arcy Spice, Beauty of Bath, Laxton's Fortune, St Edmund's Russet, Blenheim Orange and Cox's Orange Pippin. These are joined by varieties of cherries, plums, gages, medlars and quince in their season. As Andrew says, 'the most important decision of the year is to harvest the fruit on the right day. Flavour in any fruit is determined before it is picked, as is its ability to store.' The Tann family orchard is a productive and peaceful area of fifteen acres in which there is not only a wide range of fruit but also a rich variety of other plant life as well as birds, insects, bats and more.

The unassuming Crapes Fruit Farm where seasonal apples and fruit, grown on its 15 acres can be purchased. 2019

Opposite the farm is a footpath that leads across the fields towards Aldham Church. When this was built, although located near the geographical centre of the parish, only a few cottages were in close proximity to the new church, with the majority of the buildings in the parish on the main road at Fordsteet. However, since that time, there has been much building near the church and the area is now known as Aldham village.

The new church has a floor plan very similar to the old building and, although it incorporated many of the same materials and furnishings, it looked very different with its high steeple towering heavenwards and its neat flint surface work. It must have looked quite incongruous sitting in an empty churchyard lined with the ancient headstones from the former site. Time and more recent burials have mellowed the site.

Also incorporated into the new church was a marble memorial to its most famous incumbent, the Reverend Philip Morant, author of *The*

History and Antiquities of the County of Essex. This was published in the 1760s and was the first scholarly history of Essex. Written before the days of professional historians, this outstanding work by an enthusiastic amateur helped to establish later professional standards. Such is the standard of the work and presentation that it is still widely referred to today. In 1966 the Essex Archaeological Society restored and moved the stone from Philip Morant's burial place, which was in the chancel of the old church, to a place inside the new church.

As stated previously, when the location was chosen, for the new site, it was near to the geographical centre of the parish. However,

Aldham Church of St Margaret & St Catherine, which was built in 1855. 2013

*Philip Morant - historian of Essex, was
Aldham Rector from 1745 to 1770.*

this is no longer the case. This is due to the fact that the new parish of Eight Ash Green has been created from parts of several parishes including part of Aldham east of the new church. As part of the boundary of this new parish runs along a short length of the Roman River, I will talk a little about it before continuing my walk across Aldham.

Eight Ash Green was created as a new civil parish in 1947. Land was acquired from the neighbouring parishes of Aldham, Stanway, Copford and Fordham. The parish has no ancient centre and started with a scattered population of less than 600. This has since grown to over 2000 by the development of residential areas around and between its open spaces at Eight Ash Green, Daisy Green, Seven Star Green and Fordham Heath.

I leave the church to walk, in a westerly direction, along Tey road. This follows the top of the ridge between the valleys of the River Colne and Roman River. A small cluster of buildings soon comes into view. This is now called Hoe Farm, it was originally Aldham Hoo or How, from the Saxon word meaning a spur or ridge of land. This word is also incorporated in the place names of Fingringhoe and Langenhoe which we encountered near the beginning of this story.

The farm was first recorded in 1331 as Aldham Hoo; the present 19th century brick façade hides a late-mediaeval fragment of a mansion, the rest of which was probably built soon after 1554. In 1639 the house stood within a rectangular moat, parts of which remain today, although it is now dry. The associated brick-walled court, gatehouse, service buildings, farmyard and barns have either been lost or converted for other uses.

During the 17th century Joseph Sewell and his wife Emma, with their ten children, lived at Hoe Farm. Joseph was an active Quaker and held meetings at his home for several other Quaker families in North Essex. At this time all Quakers were viewed with suspicion and some were persecuted with many spending time in prison. The local

Hoe Farm, Aldham. The 19th century brick façade hides parts of timber-framed Elizabethan mansion. 2014

The access, now a public footpath at the side of the converted Hoe Farm barns soon becomes an overgrown track as it leads towards Great Tey. 2019

prison at the time was in Colchester Castle. This was where Joseph was incarcerated sometime between 1655 and 1689 but he was obviously a man true to his faith as, it is recorded, he was still holding meetings in 1694.

A public footpath continues along the ridge by following the track past Hoe Farm to the railway. This it crosses by a substantial brick bridge before becoming a footpath and descending to a minor tributary of Roman River, which marks the parish boundary. Despite the fact that the stream is often dry there is, on both sides of its course a flourishing hedge. In this, on the Aldham side, is an over-grown kissing gate that opens onto a wooden bridge and my next parish of Great Tey.

The brick bridge over the Marks Tey- Sudbury railway line where the footpath between Hoe Farm, Aldham and Great Tey crosses just before the by parish boundary. 2019

A look back at the Kissing Gate and bridge at the parish boundary between Aldham and Great Tey. 2019

CHAPTER 12

Great Tey

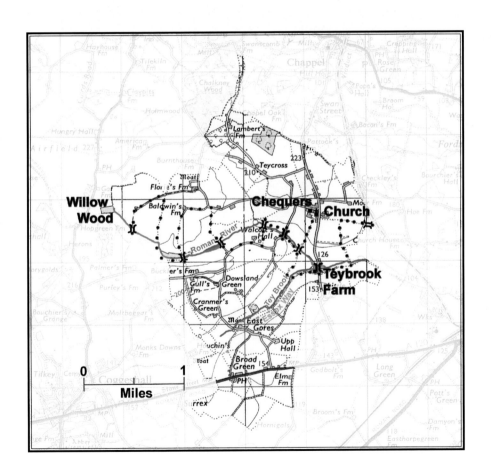

The sign, like the village is dominated by the church with its large Norman tower. The tractor and sheep represent the local farming activities, which are still important to the local community. The anvil represents the forge, which was vital for maintaining agricultural implements and shoeing horses but sadly disappeared after WWII.

Tey is thought to be derived from the Old English word 'tiege' or 'teag' meaning an enclosure. Great Tey was once called Tey a la steple because of its large church tower.

Recorded in the Domesday Book in 1086 as Tey, which consisted of Great Tey and Little Tey. After the Conquest it was held by Count Eustace and contained one mill.

In 1848 William White described Great Tey as a pleasant village of 733 inhabitants and 2478 acres. It has many scattered houses and the soil is very fertile. The Roman River has its source here.

The population of the parish of Great Tey in 2011 was 911.

216

This parish is the last on my journey. I enter it on its eastern side and the source of Roman River is on its western extremity. On the river's way through the parish it is joined by its numerous headwaters some of which I will encounter on my walk across the parish. It would be convenient to follow the headwater I have just crossed but that is not where the footpath leads. The footpath takes me up the hill towards the village centre, which I will visit later. First I will walk a little more of the river, and to this end, partway up the hill I turn to my left. A strip of phacelia, a predominantly purple crop often grown as a green manure or, as here, a forage crop for bees and other nectar loving insects borders the path, which takes me across open farmland down towards the river.

The footbridge over the swampy area of Roman River at Aldercar. 2019

The path crosses the river by a footbridge at what is shown on the map as Aldercar. This is a narrow strip of riverside woodland, which at one time could well have been dominated by alder. A carr is an area of swampy land, hence the name. The alders are now joined by a variety of other water-loving trees and shrubs.

The footpath now runs along the field edge following the river until it reaches the road at Teybrook Farm. This has long been a significant farm in the parish. Until the 16ᵗʰ century it was held by the lord of the manor. A map of 1613 shows a collection of buildings including a farmhouse with a large barn along with another barn on the other side of the road. Since then there have been many changes but this is still a working farm and many of its buildings have been re-purposed. There is an area of business units, a glamping enterprise and one of the afore-mentioned large barns has been tastefully converted into *The Barn* restaurant.

Tey Brook is one of the few named tributaries of Roman River and joins the river here at the farm. Until 1966 each flowed in its own ford across the road before their confluence. Roger Browning, a member of the third generation of his family to own the farm, objected to the removal of the fords by the Highways Authority, but sadly to no avail. Both streams now flow unseen in culverts beneath the road. The only reminders that things were ever different are a few cobbles in the road and an indignant plaque on the farm wall.

Before I leave Teybrook Farm, I will just mention a little ancient history and speculation. Colchester Archaeological Group has investigated several areas on the farm and have identified finds that indicate the site has been occupied for a very long time. Stone Age axes have been found and a Bronze Age cemetery containing fourteen burials was excavated in 2003. Several other mounds or barrows situated on the farm are yet to be investigated.

The plaque in the wall at Teybrook Farm. 2019

THE FORDS AT THIS FARM

WERE DESTROYED BY
THE HIGHWAYS AUTHORITY IN 1966

AGAINST THE WISHES OF THE
LANDOWNER R BROWNING

Tey Brook ford. The wall beyond the footbridge now bears the plaque. Early 1960s

Richard Browning

The installation of the culvert that now takes the brook beneath the road. 1964

Richard Browning

219

The site of the former Tey Brook ford. 2019

The culvert that now takes Roman River below the site of the former ford. The plaque can be seen in the wall behind. 2019

I have Mentioned crop marks before. Here on Teybrook Farm a series of linear marks appeared to cross the Tey Brook. Excavation revealed what is thought to be a three-lane Roman road that crossed the river by a ford and continued north up to where the village of Great Tey is now situated.

I am heading in a similar direction but along the footpath that leaves the farm by a small, refurbished barn and a miscellany of sheds and caravans that have morphed into a building. The path follows the Tey Brook, although a little distance from it. In 1219 the brook was recorded as Kenebrok, which means cows' brook, implying there was meadow-grazing along its banks. After passing the complex of farm

A Mesolithic (Mid Stone Age) Axe 8500 - 4500 BC found on Teybrook Farm

Richard Browning

A Neolithic (New Stone Age) Axe 4000 - 2000 BC found on Teybrook Farm

Richard Browning

A pottery burial urn from about 1200 BC (Bronze Age) uncovered by Tim Cordal on Teybrook Farm in 2003. The urn still contained cremated bone fragments. Subsequent investigation showed this was one of fourteen similar burials all surrounded by a deep, circular ditch some 26 metres in diameter.

Richard Browning

221

buildings I passed through a kissing gate into arable farmland. No livestock now; the kissing gate being the only indication that there may have been in the not-too-distant past. At the end of the field the path descends to the brook and another kissing gate, this is where my path meets the Essex Way. This is a long distance walk that crosses Essex from Epping to Harwich. It combines footpaths and lanes to create an interesting and varied 81-mile route, of which about five are within the parish of Great Tey.

I turn to the right to follow the Essex Way heading north. This goes back along the other side of Tey Brook before following the side of a wood to eventually arrive at Roman River. Here the path divides, one follows the river and the other continues as the Essex Way into Great Tey village.

Before I continue along the Roman River, I am going to stay on the Essex Way for a quarter-mile to the village. The path leads directly to the centre, which is dominated by the Church of St Barnabas. Its massive Norman tower is said to be one of the best examples in the country. Quite why the village has such a large church no one is

The Essex Way continues over the bridge; the riverside path is to the left. 2019

The Essex Way symbol is the Poppy. 2019

certain. At one time it was even larger and in 1829 the parish had to decide whether to repair what was becoming a dilapidated over-sized edifice or demolish part of it leaving a smaller structure, which would be easier to maintain. They obtained quotes for both options and chose to demolish the nave because that option was to be about half the cost of a full restoration. It turned out not to be the case. The demolition of the Norman nave and the building of the much smaller, truncated replacement ended up costing just as much as the full restoration would have been.

Although the church is renowned for its Norman tower, it stands on Saxon foundations. Many aspects of the history of England in pre-Norman times are vague and are virtually non-existent for Great Tey. But that doesn't hinder speculation. It has been said that the church is, and always has been, too large for a parish church; its size and cruciform plan is more in keeping with that of a minster. These were established during Anglo-Saxon times and were usually attached to a monastery and served an area, equivalent to that of several parishes. It has been suggested that the area consisting of Great Tey; including Chappel, which was part of Great Tey until 1352, Marks Tey, Little Tey and Aldham could have been such an area. The reason for including Aldham with the Teys is that it places Great Tey church at the geographical centre of the estate and the fact it is called Aldham, or old settlement, suggests it was a pre-existing community. Such a combined area would have contained within it areas of grazing, woodland, meadow, arable land and water, in short all the components needed for self-sufficiency.

It has been further suggested that the Saxon estate could have been a successor to an earlier Roman estate. This idea is supported by several coin finds and the unusually large amount of Roman brick used in the church building. It also provides a reason for the mysterious three-lane Roman road discovered at Teybrook Farm, leading from Stane Street up to the village.

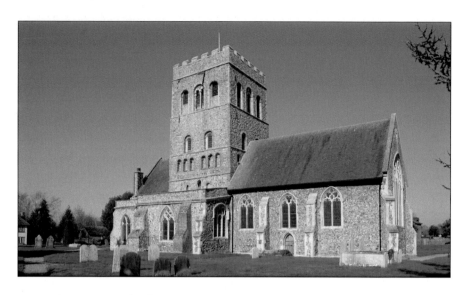

The Church of St Barnabas, Great Tey. 2019

The Church of St Barnabas before the demolition of the nave in 1829.

The combined parishes of Great Tey, Marks Tey, Little Tey, Chappel and Aldham with Great Tey church at their geographical centre.

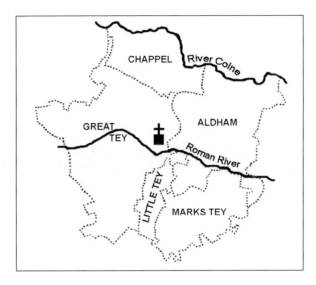

The lack of any documentary evidence could be explained if it was lost during times of turmoil or during an overwhelming Danish incursion. All in all, it seems likely that at some time during the Anglo-Saxon period some form of large estate existed, but when, and for how long, is likely to remain unknown.

In most villages the church and the pub are not far apart and Great Tey is no exception. Adjacent to the churchyard stands the 16th century *Chequers*. Originally built as a rather grand house, it is thought to have been an inn since 1660. It is not known why it is called the Chequers but inns of this name are sometimes derived from the coat of arms of a local landowner. This is obviously what the designer of the current sign thought. Other possible derivations are associated with the chequer board, which was originally used as an aid to counting and is the origin of the word exchequer; yet another is that it is derived from the common name for the wild service tree, the chequer tree, because its bark tends to flake and break up into squares. This tree was often

The Chequers *and the Church of St Barnabas. c1915*

found in or near pub gardens because, before the introduction of hops, its fruit was used to flavour beer. What is now the *Chequers* car park was at one time an orchard belonging to the property and today there is still a chequer tree not too far away.

I left the *Chequers* refreshed to retrace my steps down to Roman River. Throughout its length there are few places where a public footpath runs beside it, but in Great Tey it does so for about half-a-mile. Firstly along its southern bank, the OS Explorer map shows another H Ram here but there is no longer any trace of its existence. When in use it pumped water up to the cowshed at Warrens Farm. On to Brick Kiln Cottage where the footpath crosses the road to continue along the northern bank.

The Chequers *and the Church of St Barnabas. 2019*

The name of this cottage gives a clue to its history and its humperty bumpy garden suggests this could have been the site of the excavation of suitable clay. Unsurprisingly the road bridge at this site is built of brick. However this is not noticeable from the road, since the balustrades have long been replaced with what has become the standard on small bridges; a pair of horizontal steel bars. The brick parapets were certainly there in 1896 when the Ordnance Survey used the bench mark inscribed on the southeast corner. Today there remains a slight hump in the road as it follows the arch of the bridge.

The river, which throughout its length has seldom been much more than a stream, is now barely noticeable beneath its bourgeoning vegetation. The first part of this path is quite well walked as part of a circular route used by dog walkers. I soon reach the footbridge, which I will name Walcott's Farm Bridge, after the farm it leads to. I will do this for several more crossing places that are to follow. There is no

Above: The bridge by Brick Kiln Cottage where the riverside footpath moves from one bank to the other. The steel bar balustrade is atop a single arch brick bridge. 2018

Left: The road bridge at Brick Kiln Cottage over Roman River, the first from its source. 2018

riverside public footpath for a while, which means I hop from side to side across the now shallow valley to view the river at a succession of crossing places.

The path leads up to the road at Walcott's Farm. From here I walk the short distance along the lane to the next farm, Braziers. On this beautiful summers day I am accompanied by the shadows of butterflies as they dance along the road beside me. At Braziers, the footpath beside the farmhouse has lost its fingerpost but the gated wide track is unmistakable as it immediately drops down to the river where the track is raised to form a dam that creates a sizable, tree-lined farm reservoir. I could hear, but not see, the trickle from the overflow as the river continued its journey along the valley.

From here it was up the grass track to the lane and then along the gravel track that is a public footpath to Baldwin's Farm. From here the path descends slowly down to the river by following one of its numerous minor tributaries.

Walcott's Farm Footbridge over Roman River. 2019

The wide farm track that was built up during the 1950s to form a dam across the valley to create a sizable farm reservoir. 2019

The tree lined reservoir below Braziers on the Roman River. 2019

I don't know what I was expecting but it was not what I found. A small area of well-managed woodland with, what was now a grass track running into a glade as it crossed the diminutive Roman River. The bridge had no balustrades and looked as if it could be one of the oldest that crosses the river by what is no more than a small brick culvert.

This is the highest place along the river where I have found water all year round; which brings me to the question, where is the source? I followed the path alongside the river to the end of the wood from where the path continues up to Florie's Lane. Here I turned left and walked back down this unmade lane to meet the river a mere quarter-mile upstream; but there was no stream, the riverbed was dry. I have visited this place at all times of the year and seldom seen it wet, and never flowing, and yet the source is supposed to be on the parish boundary that runs alongside Willow Wood, which is over a quarter-mile further along.

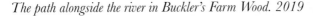

The path alongside the river in Buckler's Farm Wood. 2019

The infant Roman River sometimes flows down the ditch on the left and through a pipe under Florie's Lane. 2019

The dry riverbed as it heads away from Florie's Lane toward Buckler's Farm Wood. 2019

So, where is the source? There is no universally agreed definition for determining the source of a river. One definition of the length of a river is to measure the distance between the mouth and its most distant headwater. But that does not overcome the problem of deciding where it should be. Is it the point from which water flows all year round, or the furthest point from which water could flow, or somewhere in between? Geographers seldom pinpoint this and does it matter? In the case of Roman River, all possibilities are within a mile of each other and, I am of the opinion, it cannot really be called a river until several of its headwaters have joined together to produce a reasonable flow.

The most recent OS map shows the source on the parish boundary as it passes Willow Wood. The most accurate depiction of what I have found is that shown on an 1888 OS map which is a SP (spring) beside

Willow Wood but the Roman River is only marked as far as the wood below Buckler's Farm. This is as far as the river bed is wet for most of the year.

I have reached the source of the river and the end of my story. I have enjoyed setting down some of the discoveries I have made, and experiences I have had, during my ventures along the valley. When I began writing this book I wondered if I would find enough to write about this twelve mile, unspectacular stream, but I soon realized that I saw different things each time I walked part of it. A change in the weather or time of year changed what I saw. As did my attitude of mind. If I was looking for buildings or humps and bumps in the terrain I tended not to notice animal tracks or particular trees or plants. Sometimes I would engage with other walkers and at others pass them by. I have presented a varied selection of my discoveries and experiences in the hope that my readers will find, at least some of, them interesting. Mankind has walked this valley for thousands of years and many have settled on its banks. Some have left evidence of their occupation, which is fascinating to interpret. Many others have just passed through leaving no physical evidence, but sometimes story and myth, which I find just as fascinating to interpret. I hope you have derived as much enjoyment from reading this book as it has given me to write it.

The entrance to the wood below Bucklers.
The waters of Roman River flow from here all year round

Select Bibliography

Benham, Hervey	*Some Essex Water Mills*	
	Essex county Newspapers	1976
Boot, F & Davenport, A	*The Creation of a Village (Tiptree)*	
	WEA	1977
Brown, A F J	*Essex People 1750-1900*	
	Essex County Council	1972
Carter, H M	*Tolleshunt Knights*	
	Church Restoration Committee	1955
Crummy, P	*City of Victory*	
	Colchester Archaeological Trust	1997
Edwards, Christina	*The Parish of Stanway c1700-c1840*	
	Belhus Book	2001
Elrington, C R (Ed)	*Victoria History of Essex Volume IX*	
	Oxford University Press	1994
Fingringhoe Recorders	*Fingringhoe, Past and Present*	
	Fingringhoe Recorders	1998
Fitch, S H G	*Colchester Quakers*	
	Stanley G Johnson	1962
Free, Ken	*Camp 186, The Lost Town of Berechurch*	
	Amberley	2010
Hazell, Olive	*The Church of St Peter & St Paul, Birch*	
	Apex Publishing Ltd	2004
Hopkirk, M	*The Story of Layer-de-la-Haye*	
	Essex County Telegraph	1934
Hunter, J	*The Essex Landscape*	
	Essex Record Office	1999

Kemble	*Essex Place Names*	
	Historical Publications	2007
Lovell. Keith	*The Land of the Tolles*	
	Keith Lovell	1991
Lovell, Keith	*Town & Village Signs*	
	Keith Lovell	1998
Mason, E E	*A History of Aldham and its Churches*	
		1980
Mason, E E	*A Short History of St Andrews church, Marks Tey*	
	The Church Publishers	1968
Millatt, T B	*The Churches-Old and New-of Birch and Layer Breton*	
	TB Millatt	1963
Morant, Philip	*History and Antiquities of Essex*	
		1768
Morris, John (Ed)	*Domesday Book, Essex*	
	Phillimore	1983
Rickwood, Ken	*The Colne*	
	D Cleveland	2013
Smith, Brian S	*Tiptree in History*	
	WEA	1960
Stapleton, N J	*The Kelvedon and Tollesbury Light Railway*	
	Town & Country Press	1968
Stark, John	*125 Years of Making Jam in Tiptree*	
	Wilkin & Son Ltd	2010
Strathern, A J	*Layer Marney 1700-1900*	
	WEA	1959
White, William	*History, Gazetteer and Directory of Essex*	
		1848
Wilson, Geoffrey	*The Old Telegraphs*	
	Phillimore	1976
Wright, A J	*St Michael & All Angels, Copford*	
		1983

INDEX

Figures in **bold** refer to illustrations